Craig Groeschel has written another terrific book. I haven't stood behind him watching him make his decisions, but I've seen him stand behind the ones he's made, both the easy ones and the hard ones. These are true words from a humble guy who lives what he talks about.

—BOB GOFF, author, *New York Times* bestselling *Love Does*

Not many people can write a book that makes following God look easy. But that's exactly what Pastor Craig Groeschel has done in this down-to-earth, practical, life-giving message. This isn't just another book about decision making; it's more about the story of our whole lives that our daily decisions create. We don't have to live by chance; we can live on purpose, on course, and part of the larger story God is weaving on the earth.

—JUDAH SMITH, lead pastor, The City Church;
author, *New York Times* bestselling *Jesus Is* _____

I believe our daily choices take us into our lifelong destiny. That's why I am so excited that Craig Groeschel's book *Divine Direction* challenges us on those small choices. This book will help you to see even the smallest decisions through the lens of God's purpose as he calls you to step into his divine direction for your life.

As someone who has learned the hard way about the power of good and bad choices, the principles in *Divine Direction* really resonate with me. If you're ready to get out of your rut and make better decisions, Craig's message is a great place to start your new journey.

—DAVE RAMSEY, bestselling author;
nationally syndicated radio show host

This book by Pastor Craig Groeschel is a must-read for anyone who has been stuck not knowing what God has planned for their life or how they should be listening to his lead. I'm so thankful for people like Craig who can come alongside us with wisdom, humor, and insight!

—JEFFERSON BETHKE, author, *New York Times* bestseller *Jesus > Religion*

When I have a big decision to make, after consulting God and my wife, the first person I go to for guidance is Craig Groeschel. His God-given ability to isolate the important issues and distill biblical wisdom into action steps is second to none. *Divine Direction* is your access point to these life-changing insights.

—STEVEN FURTICK, pastor, Elevation Church;
New York Times bestselling author

Craig Groeschel has written a practical yet spiritually grounded book that is certain to help you decide on your next steps in life. In *Divine Direction*, Craig unpacks seven decisions you can make today that will influence the stories you tell in the future.

—ANDY STANLEY, senior pastor, North Point Ministries

There was once a form of capital punishment practiced in China called *ling chi*—death by a thousand cuts. None of the incisions were a big deal, but together they were lethal. In *Divine Direction*, Pastor Craig Groeschel will help you avoid living a life of a thousand cuts.

—LEVI LUSKO, senior pastor,
Fresh Life Church; author, *Swipe Right*

We often want to know what God's will is for our lives. The answer may be a little different for each of us, but *Divine Direction* will give you a great framework for finding out what *your* story can be. With simple, practical, achievable goals, Craig helps us see the little steps that make a big difference in our lives.

—KYLE IDLEMAN, author, *Grace Is Greater*

DIVINE
DIRECTION

ALSO BY CRAIG GROESCHEL

Altar Ego: Becoming Who God Says You Are

*Chazown: Define Your Vision, Pursue Your
Passion, Live Your Life on Purpose*

The Christian Atheist: Believing in God but Living as If He Doesn't Exist

Dare to Drop the Pose (previously titled *Confessions of a Pastor*)

Fight: Winning the Battles That Matter Most

*From This Day Forward: Five Commitments to Fail-
Proof Your Marriage* (with Amy Groeschel)

It: How Churches and Leaders Can Get It and Keep It

Love, Sex, and Happily Ever After (previously titled *Going All the Way*)

Soul Detox: Clean Living in a Contaminated World

#Struggles: Following Jesus in a Selfie-Centered World

Weird: Because Normal Isn't Working

What Is God Really Like? (general editor)

DIVINE
DIRECTION

7 DECISIONS / THAT WILL CHANGE YOUR LIFE

CRAIG GROESCHEL

ZONDERVAN®

ZONDERVAN

Divine Direction
Copyright © 2017 by Craig Groeschel

Requests for information should be addressed to:
Zondervan, *3900 Sparks Dr. SE, Grand Rapids, Michigan 49546*

ISBN 978-0-310-34307-3 (international trade paper edition)
ISBN 978-0-310-34899-3 (audio)
ISBN 978-0-310-34290-8 (ebook)

Library of Congress Cataloging-in-Publication Data

Names: Groeschel, Craig, author.
Title: Divine direction : seven decisions that will change your life / Craig Groeschel.
Description: Grand Rapids, Michigan : Zondervan, [2017] | Includes bibliographical
references.
Identifiers: LCCN 2016039161 | ISBN 9780310342830 (hardcover)
Subjects: LCSH: Decision making—Religious aspects—Christianity. | Discernment
(Christian theology) | Christian life.
Classification: LCC BV4509.5 .G69625 2017 | DDC 248.4—dc23
LC record available at https://lccn.loc.gov/2016039161

Craig Groeschel is represented by Thomas J. Winters of Winters & King, Inc., Tulsa, Oklahoma.

Art direction: Jeff Miller / Faceout Studio
Interior design: Denise Froehlich

First printing December 2016 / Printed in the United States of America

We can make our plans, but the
Lord determines our steps.

—PROVERBS 16:9 NLT

Contents

Small Choices

Life is the sum of all your choices.

—ALBERT CAMUS

You are one decision away from changing your life forever.

But the funny thing is you probably don't know what that one decision will be. It's natural to assume that such a big, life-changing decision would be obvious. And sometimes it is, like whether you should take a new job in another state and relocate your family. Or whether you should return to school to finish your degree. Or whether you should marry the person you've been dating for the last few months. Clearly, huge decisions like these send countless consequences rippling through your life.

But smaller choices can also have big effects. Our lives are constantly spilling into the lives of others, and theirs into ours. Like falling dominos, even our smallest decisions sometimes cascade into consequences we never could have seen coming. That's how I met my wife—not playing dominos but studying for an important exam in college.

It was a couple of days before my business management final, a class that had been ruining weekdays for me all semester. Like most of my classmates, I would've rather done *anything* else besides study for that test. So when two of my buddies invited me to a party, I seriously considered accepting. I mean, it wasn't like I had anything more important to do, right?

Reluctantly, I decided I shouldn't go to the party, opting for one last marathon study session at the library. There was no way I could have predicted how much this one, seemingly trivial decision affected the rest of my life. With papers spread all around me at a table, I was lost in thought, making notes and flipping through a business management textbook that looked more like a phone book (which would have been more interesting to read).

"Hi." The voice startled me, and I looked up and recognized a girl from one of my other classes. She had just been walking through and decided to introduce herself. We chatted for a few minutes, and eventually I turned the conversation to my newfound faith in Christ.

Even though she didn't share my beliefs, she seemed open to discussing them, so we carried our conversation over into dinner later that night. But as the spiritual topics in our discussion heated up, she cooled off. (She later told me that even though I *seemed* normal enough, during that dinner she wrote me off as some kind of religious wacko.)

Several weeks later, I bumped into this girl again in the business building, and she excitedly grabbed my arm. "Hey! I just realized—I know a girl you *have* to meet! She's weird . . . like you! She's just as overboard for God as you are!" At first I thought she was making fun of me (and probably she was), but there really was a girl. And because of her recommendation, I met Amy Fox, the woman who became my wife and the mother of our six kids.

There's an obvious lesson here: if you want to get married, skip the party and head straight to the library! (Okay, maybe that won't work for everyone, but it's certainly good advice if you want to pass business management.) Don't get me wrong, there's nothing wrong with parties in and of themselves, but in this case, I made the solid, godly decision I needed to make. And as it turned out, God used that good decision in ways I never would have imagined.

What *is* always true is that the decisions we make today determine the stories we tell about our lives tomorrow. Every day, all day, we make one small choice after another. And those choices just keep accumulating, each one woven into the rest, forming the tapestry that is our life story.

That's why this book is so important. I've never had a more practical, life-giving message to share with you. I sincerely want to help you make deliberate, godly decisions that lead you through a life full of joy and purpose. The process requires taking responsibility for the choices you make, insuring they align with God's principles, and then following through with dedicated action. One way or another, each choice you make

> The decisions we make today determine the stories we tell about our lives tomorrow.

is the decision of a lifetime, whether or not you can see where it ultimately leads. So if you want to change your life, if you want to align what you claim to believe with how you live, and if you're willing to allow God to write your life's story, this book is for you.

You are one choice away from your best decision ever.

Play It Forward

I couldn't have predicted that my acquaintance from the library would one day introduce me to the woman of my dreams. But the truth is many of our decisions lead to fairly predictable consequences. And if we learn to choose well, we can connect the dots between where we are and where we want to be. For example, most people with healthy, secure, loving marriages know that such marriages take a little work each day, every day (and sometimes more). Learning how to parent well is similar. Kids don't just magically grow into responsible, respectful people; they need loving, consistent parental role models. These same principles apply to our work. Successful careers aren't the byproduct of circumstances or luck; they are predictable, the result of hard work, dedicated focus, and calculated risktaking.

Obviously, there are exceptions. All of us can point to marriages where both people seemed to work really hard, but they ended up divorcing anyway. Kids with incredibly loving parents can still get themselves into serious trouble. Companies can go under even with great leadership. But generally, if there's a goal you want to achieve, you have to make decisions that will move you in the direction you want to go. In his excellent book *The Principle of the Path*, my friend and fellow pastor Andy Stanley puts it this way: "Direction, not intention, determines destination."

If you want to take aim at the story you want to tell, you have to make small, life-changing choices and then act on them daily. The best decision you can make is always the *next* one. Each decision should move you closer to becoming all that God made you to be, to turn your life in the direction of a story you'll be happy to share.

Most people look at others who are successful and figure they probably made just a handful of big, really important decisions. But the opposite is true. It's the small choices no one sees that result in the big impact everyone wants.

When you choose to forgive your spouse instead of holding on to resentment, no one sees that happen. But the evidence is clear in your marriage. People may tell you how great they think your kids are without ever realizing that their maturity happened over time, growing slowly out of the small decisions, daily boundaries, and tiny course corrections you planted throughout their lives. Coworkers who see you get a promotion probably have no idea how many times you had to ignore workplace politics and just keep bringing your best every day. Even your friends who attend your college graduation might not appreciate just how many late nights you spent studying while it seemed like everyone else was procrastinating or partying.

> It's the small choices no one sees that result in the big impact everyone wants.

If you could take a step back and look at your life, you'd see that every decision matters, even the little ones. Many of our daily choices happen invisibly, almost by default, like taking the same route to work every day or hopping onto social media every time we have a spare moment. Every day, we decide what to wear, where to park, when to schedule the next meeting, how to explain some report, what to eat for dinner.

Neurologists tell us that the first time we think about a decision, our brains start weighing options, eliminating one possibility after another, until we settle on one we think is our best choice in that particular moment. But after a while, for most of the tiny decisions we make every day, we don't have to think about them anymore; they just happen.

And that makes sense. Whatever consequences decisions like these have are so small that we hardly feel them. If you're like me, you wear whatever's clean and reasonably wrinkle-free, work appropriate but still comfortable. You eat whatever kind of cereal you have in the pantry (usually something your kids don't like) or whatever's in the fridge.

But it's critical to understand: these seemingly no-big-deal decisions add up over time. They become habits. And those habits have a cumulative effect, ultimately changing the story we tell about our lives.

Let me give you a few examples of things people end up doing that, if they thought about it, they never would choose to do:

- Most people who smoke never planned to become addicted to something that can kill them. They just decided to try it once to see if they liked it.

- People who end up embezzling probably didn't set it as a long-range goal to steal from their employer. More likely they began by "borrowing" a little from petty cash to pay for lunch here and there.

- People who have an affair didn't just wake up one morning and think, "My spouse won't mind if I get intimate with that hottie at the office." It started back when they lingered a little after a meeting because they were enjoying the attention of a coworker.

- Most failed entrepreneurs probably didn't include bank-ruptcy in their startup plans. They just went over budget to take a risk they didn't properly evaluate.

- People who find themselves hooked on prescription pain-killers didn't aspire to get arrested for driving under the influence and possessing illegal drugs. They were only looking for a little relief from chronic pain.

It's easy to observe problems like these and think, *I would never do such a thing!* Nobody wants to be *that* guy, the one who lost his marriage because of his secret porn addiction. No woman wants her story to include gossip, shoplifting, and alcoholism. It's tempting to think there's no way you could become addicted to cigarettes, embezzle from your employer, cheat on your spouse, overspend your corporate budget, or keep taking pain meds after the pain stops.

But the truth is you are one decision away from changing your life forever.

Your best decision ever is the one you're about to make.

Right now.

Life Is a Multiple Choice Test

The good news is that your decision of a lifetime can do more than just help you avoid the negative; it can ignite the positive, helping you to know Jesus more intimately and make choices that honor your commitment to God. It may seem like no big deal, but brown-bagging your lunch today could start you down the path that leads to living debt-free and financially secure. You could add years to your life by stopping by the gym to work out when you'd rather just go home and eat chips on the sofa while binge-watching *Doctor Who*. Simply by making a phone call or sending a text to a friend, you could get a lifeline out of the loneliness that's dragging you under waves of depression.

You may have heard that old quote, "The definition of insanity is doing the same thing over and over and expecting different results." Even when we know something is bad for us or won't turn out well, we often still do it—most often because it gives us some short-term escape or pleasure. We know we should eat better, especially if we're trying to lose weight or overcome health issues, but it's hard to follow through on that bigger goal when someone shows up at the office with fresh donuts. Most of us struggle to connect the small choices we're constantly making with the big differences we want to see in our lives.

Just so you know where I'm coming from, I believe wholeheartedly that your best decision ever is the choice to follow and serve Jesus. But that's not just some one-time decision that you never think about again except on Sundays. Although people who ask Jesus into their lives can often remember when they made that decision, we still must continue making daily, moment-by-moment choices to deny ourselves and follow him.

Even if you don't believe in Jesus the way I do, you still have to make decisions every day just like everyone else, so I hope you'll continue reading with an open mind.

It may sound cliche, but I believe that Jesus truly can change the course of your story for all eternity. Now, I know you might be thinking, *Jesus-blah-blah-blah! Been there, done that,* especially if you've grown up around hypocritical churchgoers and lukewarm Christians. (I know because I've been there.) But that's not what I'm talking about. I want to challenge you, to invite you to look past your selfie-centered way of thinking, to get really gut-level honest with yourself.

If you feel empty, like you're always looking for something more, then you're standing at the crossroads of a divine direction. If you have tons of "friends," "followers," and "likes," but you still feel a raw longing, you know something needs to change. Maybe that's why you picked up this book. Maybe that's exactly what God wants for you. If you'll open your heart, I believe God will gently lead you, step by step, decision by decision, perhaps not to the life you've always wanted but to the life that he's always wanted for you.

He loves you so much that he lets you choose.

> If you'll open your heart, I believe God will gently lead you, step by step.

The Choice Is Yours

Ultimately it's up to you to decide what you believe, who you want to live for, and what you're going to stand for. I believe I can help you, by giving you the tools you need to make divinely inspired decisions, the ones you're facing every single day of your life from here forward.

No matter where you happen to be in your life right now, the next life-altering decision you're facing is unique to you. Maybe you've already committed to trust Jesus with your life, and now you realize that you need to make some important decisions about relationships, about whether to start a family, about switching careers, or about moving to another state. The ideas I'll present in this book will help you think about how you can make all of your decisions align with your faith and deepest values.

Throughout this book, we'll seek God's wisdom together on how you can make the best decisions in seven key areas. Each area begins with one primary decision that will help you live the story you want to tell. Even more important, changing how you make decisions will help you tell the story that *God* wants you to tell.

When you start making one divine decision after another, you'll see your story emerge, the one that God wants to tell through you. And with his help, you'll use the powerful freedom he's given you to transform your life.

If you don't like the way your life is going, the good news is that God can get things working together for your good. (See Rom. 8:28.) He's committed to you, and he wants so much more for you than you're probably settling for now. You can't change your past, but God can help you rewrite your story and change your future.

God is focused not on your happiness but on your pursuit of Jesus, which satisfies your soul like nothing else.

He did not create you to live out a tragedy, always struggling, only to end up defeated because of a few bad decisions. (Or maybe even just one.) No, he made you to live your life to the fullest, to trust him to redeem your pain with his power. God is focused not on your happiness but on your pursuit of Jesus, which satisfies your soul like nothing else.

So if you're ready to get started, the best decision you can make now is to turn the page.

1 Start

Nobody can go back and start a new
beginning, but anyone can start
today and make a new ending.

—MARIA ROBINSON

*O*seola *dragged the wet clothes from the washer into a basket*
to carry them out to the line in the back yard. As the morning
summer sun kept inching higher, she knew it wouldn't take long
for them to dry. She also knew it wouldn't take long for her little
house to heat up like an oven. Which meant she'd better get to that
ironing before it got any hotter.

She had set up her ironing board on her little screened-in
porch, both for the shade and in the hope of catching a breeze now
and then. She hunted through the clean, dry stack from an earlier

load and selected a blue Oxford dress shirt monogrammed with the initials of a local banker. He was a good man, one of her best clients. She took great pride in her work, determined to make a difference in her customers' lives by helping them look their best in fresh, spotless, perfectly pressed shirts, pants, and dresses.

As she ironed, she smiled, recalling a conversation she'd had the previous week with the banker while he was wearing this blue shirt. She had gone to deposit a little money into her savings account, and the banker had greeted her like family. He invited her to take a seat while he looked over her accounts.

After a minute, he let out a long, low whistle. "Why, Ms. McCarty, you have more money in this bank than I do! Don't you ever spend any of it on yourself?"

She laughed and shook her head. "There's nothin' I need. God is good to me, and he provides everything I could ever want. No sir, I'm savin' my money for a special purpose he's laid on my heart."

"And what would that be?" he asked. The banker expected Ms. McCarty to say she hoped for a bigger house or a cruise or maybe a shopping spree in Memphis or Atlanta.

"Well, I want to set up a scholarship fund at the university for young people who can't afford to go there. I never was able to get an education myself, but I sure do appreciate the value of one. And I want to help some young women and men have that opportunity I never got."

The memory faded as she turned the shirt over and over, carefully smoothing it with the steaming iron. She had started saving pennies and nickels and dimes as a little girl, and by the time she was a young woman, she was saving whole dollars. She had worked *as a laundress most of her life, washing and ironing the clothes of people from all over Hattiesburg, the small city she called home in southern Mississippi. Oseola knew her nature was frugal, but she also knew her habit of saving just a little each week would make a profound difference in people's lives long after she left this earth to be with the Lord.*

She chuckled, content in the pleasure she found in using her small habit to touch people she would never meet. She folded the blue shirt and hummed an old gospel hymn as she set it aside and lifted out the next one.

1.1 What's Your Story?

In the beginning . . .

Once upon a time . . .

It was a dark and stormy night . . .

Each of our stories has a unique beginning. My story started differently than yours, and yours began differently than everyone else's. But regardless of how our stories began, each of us lives out the story of our life every day.

If you're like me, you don't stop very often to think about "the story of my life." You're too busy living it! But recognizing the pattern of events in your life, the ebbs and flows of your story, can make a huge difference, both in your future and in how your story ultimately ends. Because when you understand the negative ways your past may be influencing your present, you have the power to make different choices, better choices. Reflection may also give you a clearer understanding about which things in your life you can change and which things you can't. And this prayerful reflection can become a guide to making wise and God-honoring decisions as you move forward.

If someone asked you to tell your story, what would you say? You might start with where you were born and how you were raised. You might describe your favorite teacher, your first crush, your first car. You might include that time you scored the winning touchdown or that *other* time you threw up right before singing your first solo. Maybe you'd mention the big move your family made or when you left home to go to college. If you're married, you might describe how you met your spouse. And if you're not married, you might describe the kind of person you hope to meet one day. If you're a parent, you might scroll through some photos on your phone or tablet and show off your family. Or maybe you'd discuss your latest promotion at work or when you hope to finally launch your own business.

Most of what you tell other people probably sounds pretty good. Maybe you're proud of your story. You've overcome some obstacles. You've survived some challenges. You've accomplished some goals.

Sure, you haven't been perfect or lived a flawless life, but who has? You've made your share of mistakes. (Lord knows we all have.) Some decisions you got right, and others . . . well, let's just say they're not as easy to discuss. You've had lapses of judgment. If you're like most people, you've made emotional decisions you regret.

Chances are you might have some chapters in your story

you'd rather not share with anyone. You might have secrets. You might have done things you wish you'd never done. I know I have. Though I'm not proud of it, I've lost my temper and wounded people I love with my hurtful words too many times to count. I've given in to my selfish, sinful desires and let down God, myself, and others. I've neglected my family at times, giving too much of my heart to the church. Now that two of my daughters are grown and married, I'd give anything to have more time with them at home. And these are just a few of my regrets. I've got many more I'd rather not put in print.

Maybe you've ended up somewhere you never wanted to be. You didn't mean to blow it, but you did. You made decisions that took you farther than you ever intended to go. You did some things that cost you more than you ever thought you'd have to pay. You hurt people. You compromised your values. You broke promises. You did things you can't undo. There are no do-overs like when you were a kid on the playground.

Sometimes you skip over those dark chapters of your life. Other times you embellish your stories on the fly, making a version you like better than the truth. You brush past the ugly parts and tell the happier highlights. When you're honest, you know that the truth about your story weaves all of your decisions together: some good, some not so good, and some still uncertain.

No matter how you describe your story, there's good news. Your story is not over. It's not too late to change the story that you'll tell one day. Regardless of what you've done (or haven't done), your future is still unwritten. You have more chapters to write, more victories to win, more friends to meet, more of a difference to make, more of God's goodness to experience. Even though you may not like the plot so far, with God's help, you can transform your story into one you're not ashamed to share. You can start something new.

> It's not too late to change the story that you'll tell one day. You can start something new. No matter how desperate, uncertain, afraid, or stuck you may feel right now, your story isn't over.

While events cannot be unwritten, they can be redeemed. No matter how desperate, uncertain, afraid, or stuck you may feel right now, your story isn't over. You may think your story is tragic or unbelievable or horrific or boring or funny, but you don't know how it ends. It's not too late to change.

Your best decision is the next one that will help you be the person God created you to be.

1.2 Start Where You Are

Just last week I talked to a buddy who made a tragic mistake. Just one. And it cost him more than he ever imagined. On a business trip away from his family, he had a couple of drinks with a client at dinner. Instead of going back to his hotel room afterward, he decided to head to the bar for just one more glass of beer. But one glass turned into two, and two turned into too many. Feeling buzzed and strangely adventurous, he started up a conversation with a lady who was also drinking alone. I'm sure you can figure out what happened next.

My broken friend looked at me with a distant, lifeless look in his eyes, and he said, "You know I love my wife. You know I do." His head dropped into his hands. "How could I be so stupid? I made one mistake. One stupid mistake, and now I'm going to lose everything I love."

I've heard it said that two of the biggest mistakes you can make in life are not starting and not finishing. If you're like most people, you've had good intentions to start new habits. It's a pretty safe bet that many of those good intentions you never followed through on. And it's probably likely that even the things you *did* start, many you never finished. I know what that's like. Regret sets in, and you don't feel successful. You don't feel disciplined. Sometimes you even feel like a failure.

It goes without saying that you can't travel back in time and start your life over. But there is something you *can* do, and you can do it today: you can start a new discipline that will make for a new and better ending to your story. Any day you choose, you can start something new and allow God (the finisher of your faith) to help you complete what he called you to start.

I've noticed that so many people think a successful life is made up of just a few big decisions. Starting that new business. Moving to a new city. Inventing an all-new product line. Writing that movie script. Big decisions are important, but a truly meaningful life doesn't happen through a few big decisions; you build it by stacking hundreds and hundreds of smaller ones. Vincent van Gogh nailed it when he said, "Great things are done by a series of small things brought together."

> Any day you choose, you can start something new and allow God (the finisher of your faith) to help you complete what he called you to start.

Remember the story I shared at the beginning of this chapter?

Oseola McCarty dropped out of school at an early age and worked most of her life doing other people's laundry in Hattiesburg, Mississippi. As an uneducated African American woman growing up before the Civil Rights Movement, she had few opportunities for advancement. Her life was incredibly challenging. Yet she savored each day, worked hard, and loved the Lord. During her lifetime, she saved more than $150,000, which she donated to create a scholarship fund for financially challenged students at the University of Southern Mississippi. Ms. McCarty's story proves that starting small can lead to a big positive difference in the lives of many people. The example she set shows that a great life is built on small disciplines and wise decisions.

In this chapter, we're going to prayerfully allow Jesus to show us what we need to start in order to finish well. We'll focus specifically on life-altering disciplines and habits. I'm not going to ask you to think about following your dreams or beginning a new life mission. I don't want you to think about starting a business, writing a book, or launching a ministry. We'll get to those types of decisions in chapter 4.

We're going to start small. But don't be discouraged. Most great ministries start small. Most great businesses had humble beginnings. Even the best marriages usually start with a simple hello. In the Bible, Zechariah says, "Do not despise these small beginnings, for the LORD rejoices to see the work begin" (Zech. 4:10 NLT).

If you try to focus now on the last chapter of your story, you'll likely find yourself too paralyzed to write the first page. If you try to imagine the end, it seems too grand, so distant, so ideal that you won't know where to begin. The dream will remain just that: only a dream. That's why we're going to take just one small step in the direction of the dream.

Let's say you want to tell the story of running a marathon. Can you go out and run one today? Unless you've already been training for months, the answer is no. But you can start to jog (or even walk) twenty minutes a day. That's one small step in the direction of the end of your story. If you want to preach to thousands of people, can you do that today? Not likely. But can you write one message a week to learn your way around the Bible? Of course you can! If you want to produce a major motion picture, can you do that by Christmas? No way. But you can start making short films with whatever camera you have or can borrow. You can write at least a few lines of your story.

I like to say it this way: I will do today what I *can* do to enable me to do tomorrow what I can't do today. Mother Teresa reminded us to be "faithful in the small things because it is in them that your strength lies."

> Each decision you make, no matter how small it may seem, can have a huge impact.

1.3 Flossing and Turning

Positive disciplines in a person's life usually pave the way for myriad other positive disciplines. Certain good habits create other good habits. The opposite is also true. The absence of strategic habits generates bad habits. An undisciplined life never leads to productivity or progress. If you don't put the right disciplines in place, one day you're going to find yourself telling a story you never wanted to tell.

- I was planning on it, but I never got around to it.
- I should have tried it, but now it's too late.
- I never thought I'd end up here. I wish I could do it all over again.
- Why didn't I at least try? Now look where I am in life.

I've taught in leadership settings and in the book *From This Day Forward* what I call the Flossing Principle. To the delight of dental hygienists everywhere, I tell people they must never quit flossing. Then I explain how flossing is an essential discipline in my life. Flossing likely won't be as important to you as it is to me. And my message isn't that I want you to have healthy gums. I do, but what I'm trying to convey is that we all must develop and maintain important habits because they trigger other right behaviors. And their absence triggers wrong behaviors.

An undisciplined life never leads to productivity or progress.

Why is flossing so important to me? Because it's the first and easiest discipline for me to quit. I've never liked flossing (probably because I hate being told I *have* to do something). One time my dentist quoted to me my own teaching. "You know, Craig, the decisions you make today determine the story you'll tell tomorrow. What story do you want to tell? One with all your teeth? Or one with rotten gums and your teeth falling out?"

I couldn't argue because he was using my own words against me, and also because he was holding a sharp instrument in my mouth. But that same evening, I started flossing before bed. I still don't enjoy it. When I'm tired, I'd rather just brush my teeth and fall into bed. No harm done, right? But my choosing not to floss opens the door for other problems.

When I force myself to floss, even though I don't want to, I feel disciplined. Since I feel disciplined, I continue with my workout plan. Since I work out, I eat better. I sleep better too. And when I sleep well, I wake up early and do my Bible reading before work. Then I go to work in a good frame of mind and I'm more productive. People applaud my good work, so I come home in a good mood and kiss my wife. And that's why we have six kids together.

On the other hand, when I don't floss, I don't feel disciplined. When I break the momentum of my discipline, I'm more tempted to drop other habits as well. Since I didn't floss, I'm more likely to skip a workout, which then helps me rationalize eating more junk food. Those lazy, sloppy habits then come back to haunt me when I don't sleep as well at night. I toss and turn, then wake up tired, grumpy, and even more apathetic. Since I don't feel well, I skip my Bible study, falling even deeper into my self-made pit. When I'm at work, I'm not in a good frame of mind, so I'm not as productive and I get easily distracted. Since I'm not as focused as usual, I have to work late to get everything done. Knowing that Amy won't be happy I'm late coming home, I speed down back roads, only to be pulled over by a police officer who's waiting patiently for a speeder like me. I don't want to get a speeding ticket, so I try to outrun him, only to be stopped just a block from my house by four other police officers who've set up a roadblock.

Then my mug shot ends up on the ten o'clock news, and I spend the night in jail—all because I didn't floss.

Okay, so maybe I'm exaggerating. A little. But you have to agree: certain disciplines lead to other positive actions.

And the path to discipline begins with your daily decisions.

1.4 Overnight Success

Behind every great story there's always another story. Rarely does success come without time, discipline, and hard work. Successful people often joke that they spent years becoming an overnight success. What many don't realize is that it's the things no one sees that result in the things everyone wants. It's the faithfulness to do mundane things well, to develop productive habits, and to remain faithful that eventually leads to success.

Old Testament prophet Daniel is a great example of this. Whether you know a lot or a little about Daniel, when you hear his name, you probably think, *Oh, yeah . . . Daniel in the lions' den.* Any kid who grew up attending Sunday school or visiting vacation Bible school has heard the amazing story of Daniel surviving the night in a cave filled with hungry felines.

It's the things no one sees that result in the things everyone wants.

Let me refresh your memory, and then we'll go back to the part many overlook. King Darius was the reigning king of Persia. As his kingdom grew, he appointed 120 satraps (similar to our present-day state governors) to handle regional matters and help govern the people. The king then chose three administrators to oversee those 120 satraps. Daniel was one of the chosen leaders. Over time, by consistently serving the king with an excellent spirit, Daniel stood out among all the other satraps and administrators. Eventually the king decided to place Daniel in charge of the entire kingdom.

So Daniel was an overnight success, right? Actually, nothing could be farther from the truth. Don't forget, there's a story behind every story. Why was Daniel successful? Why was he favored above others? Why did the king respect him so much? Promote him so quickly? Believe in his leadership? Why did God look favorably on Daniel? Why did God close the mouths of the meat-eating lions?

We find our answers in a part of Daniel's story that many people skim over. His divine favor was the result of one small decision he made at some point in his life. We don't know when Daniel made this decision or why. We don't know whether someone helped him or he decided it on his own. All we know is that Daniel made one decision, starting one habit that changed his story.

As you might expect, the other leaders were fuming with jealousy of Daniel. The story continues, "At this, the administrators and the satraps tried to find grounds for charges against Daniel in his conduct of government affairs, but they were unable to do so. They could find no corruption in him, because he was trustworthy and neither corrupt nor negligent. Finally these men said, 'We will never find any basis for charges against this man Daniel unless it has something to do with the law of his God'" (Dan. 6:4–5).

Let's consider for a moment some of the great qualities of our hero Daniel. Even though the other guys did everything they could to find something wrong with him, they couldn't find anything. Daniel was honest, trustworthy, and dependable in all that he did. He was exactly the type of person the king was looking to promote. So his opponents decided there was only one way they could trap Daniel into doing something worthy of punishment. They needed to devise a plan that involved his faith in God. They knew he wouldn't do anything wrong. They were going to have to back him into a spiritual corner.

"So these administrators and satraps went as a group to the king and said: 'May King Darius live forever! The royal administrators, prefects, satraps, advisers and governors have all agreed that the king should issue an edict and enforce the decree that anyone who prays to any god or man during the next thirty days, except to you, Your Majesty, shall be thrown into the lions' den'" (vv. 6–7). The king apparently liked the sound of their plan because he agreed to their proposal. No one could pray to anyone but him for the next month. And so the plan to trap Daniel was set in motion.

When Daniel heard about the new thirty-day restriction on prayer, he did the same thing he'd done three times a day for months, maybe years, possibly decades. Daniel went to his house and prayed to God.

As a result, Dan the Man was arrested and had to stare down the big cats and prove that God was his one and only. But think for a minute. It wasn't just that Daniel wasn't afraid of lions or had some super courage that mere mortals can never hope to attain. No, Daniel had started a regular practice much earlier in his life that helped him face this impossible situation. To others, prayer might have seemed insignificant. But to Daniel, it was a discipline that shaped his story.

We don't know how many years Daniel had been practicing this habit, but three times a day, every day, Daniel stopped and looked toward heaven. He worshiped God. He aligned his heart with God's heart. He sought God's will to be done through his life. Because of Daniel's consistent and prayerful focus, he grew as a God follower, as a person, and as a leader.

Daniel wasn't an overnight success. He was able to stand tall because he'd faithfully knelt before the one true king. The small, daily discipline of prayer equipped him to face the big, scary test of those hungry lions, both the peers who were attempting to destroy him as well as the big cats in the arena. Starting something small and then faithfully continuing it made his story so rich that it's been told for thousands of years now, and still counting.

1.5 Author and Finisher

How do you start something that will help you face the lions in your life? The best way to find a meaningful framework for your story is to pursue an eternal perspective. What story do you think God wants you to tell about your life? When you look into your future, where do you think God wants you to be? What does God want you to want? For now, don't worry about the distance between you and the end of your story. But if you think about what your future should be, you can have some sense of what direction you need to head in.

Chances are you can think of something right now that you know God would love to include in your story. Maybe you're strapped financially, but you know it would honor God for you to tell the story of how you escaped from the bondage of debt to become a blessing to others. If Oseola McCarty's example inspires you, maybe you could change your story to something like this:

Several years ago, I was drowning in debt. Then one day I decided to start a budget [or take a class or read a book or whatever]. It wasn't easy, but I paid off first one credit card, then another. Before long, I paid off my car, then my student loans. Today I'm debt free except for the house, and I'm on track to have that paid off in less than four years. I don't just tithe anymore; my new financial freedom allows me to give generous offerings whenever I feel God's Spirit prompting me to.

Or maybe your story could involve changing your priorities. You know whether the story you're telling now is off track. But if you let God help you author your story, it might one day go something like this:

Years ago I was so into my career that I was missing out on what was most important in life. I thought I was providing a better life for my family, but in reality I was pursuing selfish dreams and neglecting those I loved the most. That's when I decided to get home every evening by six o'clock [or stop taking work home or change careers or whatever]. Now my marriage is better than it's ever been. I haven't missed one of my children's dance recitals or T-ball games in over two years. This is the way life was supposed to be. Now I work to live, not the other way around.

It could be that you know you aren't properly caring for your body, the temple of the Spirit of God. You don't eat right. You rarely exercise. You are often stressed. You know God wants something different for you, so you decide to change your story. One day your story could be something like this:

When I realized I wasn't honoring God with my body, I decided to start working out daily [or hire a trainer or start a diet or begin walking or whatever]. I know it's hard to believe, but I used to weigh about thirty pounds more than I do today. I feel better now than I ever have before.

Perhaps your family is a Christian family, but you aren't really growing in your faith or making a difference in this world. You know God wants more of your heart. Your story might go something like this:

Several years ago, we believed in God, but we didn't know him intimately, and we didn't serve him passionately. One day we decided to make God our family's top priority. We committed to attend church [or join a small group or read the Bible together or get involved in a ministry or whatever]. Now our whole family is doing our best to glorify Christ in all we do. Our kids are bold in their faith. We're very involved in our church. And we can tell that we're making a difference serving every week in local ministry outreach. Now we don't just believe in God, but our lives revolve around serving him.

Consider what might happen if you remember to floss tonight or work out tomorrow morning or not skip church this Sunday or spend some special time with someone you love. A small decision today could even change your near future. It doesn't always take a long time to see big differences in your life. What story do you believe God wants you to tell five or ten years from now? What does God want you to want? Jot down your thoughts about what you believe God wants for your future. It doesn't have to be perfect. You don't have to commit to what you write just yet. Just capture on paper the thoughts that come to mind.

1.6 Just One Thing

After you have a sense of what God wants you to want, where do you begin? What discipline do you need to start practicing to head toward where God wants you to get? Just one thing. You'll be tempted to pick three, four, or even ten, but don't. Whatever you do, pick just one thing. Because if you pick more than one, you likely won't achieve any of them. But if you select just one, you can absolutely start writing the story God wants you to write.

For most of my adult life, I've started one new discipline each year. Some were just little things in my day or week; others took some real work. While this may not seem like much change, over five years I added five new disciplines to my life. Over a decade I added ten. And each one is locked in. While I'm still far from perfect, my life is richer and more enjoyable, and my story is closer to where God wants it to be. Just imagine how different your story would be if over the next ten years you added ten God-centered disciplines to your life.

Let me share a few of the disciplines I started over the years and how they have changed my story. I grew up in a lower-middle-class home. We never went without the basics, but we never had a lot left over to help others. I decided that I wanted to have financial flexibility so our family could be generous to others. So in my early twenties, I set aside the first ten percent of my income to give to God and the next ten percent to invest.

Month after month, I put God first and investment in my future second. Many months this discipline was very difficult, but I never faltered. Investing ten percent doesn't sound like a lot, especially when your income isn't much, and mine wasn't. But consistency over time with compounding interest made a difference. My small monthly investments added up—way up. Now we're able to live on a fraction of our income, debt free, giving freely—all because I decided to set aside a percentage of income early in life. My story is different because of this one small discipline.

Early in ministry, I found the hours of church work grueling. No matter how much I was doing, I always thought I could call on more people, train more volunteers, and study more for a message. I was convinced that I was too busy to take care of myself, so exercising was out of the question. Then one day a trusted mentor told me I was too busy *not* to exercise. "If you don't take care of yourself," my mentor explained compassionately, "you won't be much good to others." So I decided to start working out. I picked a friend to join me. Twenty years later, I still work out with the same friend, and I'm in good physical shape.

Like many people I know, I've always battled with working

more than I should. Even though this behavior may be applauded by those who work with you, it is frowned on at home. Years ago I told my daughter I'd be home later to kiss her goodnight. She looked at me innocently and said, "Daddy, this isn't your home. You live at the office." That's when I decided to go to counseling for my workaholic tendencies. With the help of a good counselor, I changed. One day when my children tell their story, I'll be a part of it because I chose to limit how much I work to focus on what matters most. This is a part of my story that I'll never regret.

Just two years after I became a Christian, I entered full-time ministry in the church. I didn't know the Bible well at all. I was very insecure, constantly worried that how little I knew might be keeping me from helping people the way I should, and possibly even dishonoring God. I decided to read through the Bible once each year. I can't remember how many years ago I started doing this. Now I'm certainly no Bible scholar, but I do know the Bible a hundred times better than if I had never started this discipline.

Thankfully, I was blessed with a good marriage right from the start. All of my friends know I married up—*way* up. And even though we've always been close, one day Amy told me that she desired more spiritual intimacy. Thanks to her encouragement, I decided we should start consistently praying together as a couple. (Believe it or not, this wasn't easy for me—and I'm a pastor!) But that one discipline made our good marriage even better. You'd be amazed how much God can change your marriage when you seek him together daily.

I'd like to tell you about just one more "one thing." Several years ago, I noticed that ministry had become more of a strain on me than a joy. I felt like I was doing the work in my own strength, not depending on God as I should. So I decided to devote the first twenty-one days of each new year to him, denying myself my normal food, fasting and seeking God. This wasn't just difficult; at first it was a great burden. But I cannot put into words how real the presence of God became to me through this process. For the last several years, our entire church staff has joined me, along with many people who attend our church, in seeking God with a fast every January. More than just my story, the story of our entire church is different because we decided to fast together.

Ever since I started seeking God through fasting, I can sense his voice more clearly. His Word is more alive to me than ever before. Consistent fasting even reveals to me things in my life that need to be cleansed.

Sometimes it's hard for me to keep track of all of my feelings, everything I learn each day, and all the questions I think of that I'd like to take to God. So this year, I started journaling. I know a lot of people who have tried to journal, only to eventually give up. That won't happen to me. How do I know? Because I'm keeping it simple. I've committed to write at least one sentence a day. That's it. Just one sentence. So far, what I've found is that just one sentence can quickly lead to two, which then often flows into several paragraphs. But that's not the goal I set. By aiming for something achievable, I'm in the process of building yet another discipline that is helping to shape the story that my life is telling.

All of those one things became parts of my story. Don't let the thought of them overwhelm you. Big changes are possible; they just may not happen overnight. Remember, it's just one decision to start something each year. You can do that. With God's help, you know you can.

As I am writing this, I can't help reflecting on my choices. How much different would my life be if I had never decided to start those disciplines? What if I didn't invest? I might be living paycheck to paycheck. What if I didn't make exercise a priority? I might be overweight, out of shape, or worse. What if I didn't get counseling for my problem of overworking? Would my family be in a shambles today? What if Amy and I hadn't prayed together? Would we have drifted apart? Or worse? What if I didn't make God's Word a daily priority? Who knows what I could have done to destroy my life? What if I didn't fast? Would I still be doing ministry in my own strength? Limiting what God wanted to do in me and through me?

1.7 Ready, Set, Start

There's an interesting story in the Old Testament about one of the leaders of Israel, King Ahab. A prophet explained that God would change Israel's story by giving the enemy army into the hands of the Israelites. Ahab just couldn't see it. He asked, "But who will do this?"

The prophet answered him, "This is what the LORD says: 'The junior officers under the provincial commanders will do it.'"

"And who will start the battle?" he asked.

The prophet answered, "You will" (1 Kings 20:14).

Think about the king's second question: "Who will start the battle?" The prophet boldly replied, "You will!" If we want to see what God will accomplish, we have to move toward him.

God will finish it, but you have to start it.

So what's your one thing? What one discipline do you need to start so that you can write the story God wants you to write?

Maybe you know you need to grow spiritually. Don't just think about it and feel bad about it. Do something about it. Perhaps you will commit to worship at church every week. Or maybe you'll decide to read through the Bible every year. Or you might join a small group or start serving in your church or start volunteering with a local missions group.

Do you need to grow as a leader? Improve as a mom? Grow as a husband? Maybe you should start learning from a mentor or begin praying daily about your need or start reading an article a week about the thing you want to get better at.

It might be that you need to get your finances under control. You're sick of swimming in debt, tired of worrying about money. Maybe it's time you started going to a Dave Ramsey class or got help creating a budget or began giving so you can break your grip on getting.

If your marriage isn't what it should be, what do you need to start so you can change the story of your marriage? Maybe it's time you started praying together daily or reading the Bible together or simply going out together once a week with no kids.

What one thing do you need to begin?

Now's a good time to jot down something you need to start. Walk over to your desk and get a pen and paper to record your thoughts. Don't overthink this. But do take a moment to get it down on paper. Just a sentence or two.

If you have a lot of ideas and you're not sure where to begin, I'm going to help you decide. Look at your phone or a clock and check the time. Did you do it? Good. Now, you have twenty-four hours to decide on one thing.

Think about it.

Pray about it.

Talk about it.

Sleep on it.

Think some more briefly tomorrow and then commit. You don't need weeks to come up with your one thing. By this time tomorrow, you will make your decision. And just like Daniel's decision to pray began the future story he'd tell, you'll begin writing the story that God wants you to tell.

Don't just think, *That's a great idea, Craig. It sounds really nice. I'll try that sometime*, and then put it off.

> **There is no better time to start writing your future story than right now.**

There is no better time to start writing your future story than right now. The famous and very prolific Walt Disney said, "The way to get started is to quit talking and start doing." Today is a better day to start than tomorrow. If you don't start now, a year from now you'll wish you had.

Who's going to start it?

You will.

Start a discipline today that will change your story forever.
Just start where you are.
Just take that first step.
Just one step.

2 Stop

Stop. Revive. Survive.

—MELINA MARCHETTA

*H*e was a smart guy. He knew God had blessed him with a gift for making money. He also knew he should feel happier than he did most days. After all, he was making $250,000 a year now, his net worth was in the seven-figures range, and he wasn't even thirty yet. He was deeply in love with his beautiful wife, a woman who believed in him and supported the intelligent risks he was taking in real estate. He was a college graduate, an active member of a great church, and a respected young businessman. He and his wife hoped to start a family soon, and they'd already started planning their dream house.

So what if he played his business deals fast and loose sometimes? Nothing he was doing was illegal, unethical, or, as far as he knew, unbiblical. He was just playing the game, doing business the same way he saw everybody else doing it. If he found great properties guaranteed to make a profit and his bank was willing to extend a loan for his company to buy them, he figured he was living the American dream.

Then one day a friend at the bank called him with bad news. They had merged with another bank, and the new bank officers were examining lending practices and client loans. They were planning to call in all his short-term loans. With a single phone call, he was sunk.

Sure enough, it wasn't long before the bank demanded immediate payment of more than a million dollars. Frantic, he begged for an extension, but soon it became clear that he was going to be forced into bankruptcy. All of his hard work down the drain, all for nothing.

It seemed like his story was over before it even got very far.

But he refused to let the bankruptcy kill his dream. And he knew that if he was going to be successful, he was going to have to stop the business practices that had gotten him into trouble. Even if they weren't illegal or unethical, he realized they weren't sound stewardship, a word he'd heard in church many times but was only now beginning to understand.

So he worked hard. He studied every financial training resource he could get his hands on. He sought out people who had a lot of money and asked them questions about their habits. He researched banks, loans, credit practices, state and federal laws,

*and especially what he had grown to consider the ultimate author-
ity on all subjects, the Bible.*

*Soon he sensed God calling him back into business, and even
back into real estate, but this time with one crucial difference: he
knew that God wanted him to help others understand the principles
he'd been embracing and to teach them about true stewardship.*

*Then he began living the story he wanted to tell, the one he
knew God wanted him to tell. Not only did his financial crisis force
him to change his goals and business practices, he also chose to
stop the habits that had led to them. He realized his desire to be
a good steward not just with money but with everything that God
had entrusted to him.*

2.1 Up on the Roof

No matter how old we get, wisdom often hangs in the balance
between a good decision and a slippery slope toward disaster. In
my case, this is often literally true. Or at least it was recently when
I injured my foot in a savage game of indoor soccer. Immediately
after it happened, I could barely walk. My doctor gave me a giant,
heavy, ugly boot that I had to wear while my foot healed, a sort
of "man-UGG."

I was a good patient—until the day that I remembered we still
had Christmas lights up on our house. And since it was almost
Valentine's Day and I didn't want to be that guy who leaves his
Christmas lights up all year, I decided they needed to come
down—right then.

So I did what any reasonable, responsible adult with only one healthy leg would do: I dragged my extension ladder out of the garage and hobbled with it to the side of the house. I needed an accomplice who wouldn't ask too many questions, so I enlisted the most highly qualified member of my family: nine-year-old Joy.

What should have been a straightforward, one-hour job sprawled into two. Even so, I was feeling pretty good about my progress until I realized the last string went up the side of the garage to the second story, along the steepest part of our roof. Even under ideal circumstances, this scenario would inspire its own famous last words: "But it didn't look that high!"

But we were so close to being finished. I vowed to get it done and dragged myself up onto the roof. Then I belly-crawled up this lethal slope. Honestly, it would have been risky even with two healthy feet. Somehow I inched myself all the way to the top. I stopped to catch my breath and have a look around.

Now, I'm no physics major, but I did some quick figuring, and according to my calculations, if a person of my height and weight and age $(H + W + A)$ fell off a roof of this grade $(\wedge)$, they'd most likely burst open like a pinata when they hit the ground $(H + W + A) + (\wedge) = (splat)^2$.

I took a deep breath, gathered my courage, told my common sense to mind its own business, and scooted toward the strand of lights. Almost immediately, my giant immobile foot slipped and dragged me down like an anchor. Sliding at a speed faster than I could calculate, I dug my forearms into the asphalt shingles for all I was worth. It cost me a lot of skin and blood, but by the grace of God I stopped about halfway down.

Gasping and bleeding, I lay there at a forty-five-degree angle considering my options. The voice of reason finally broke through from below.

"Daddy, you know I love you. But I don't think this is a very good idea!"

Joy's concern jolted me back to reality. I was finally able to stop myself and ask, Where does my story go from here?

Best possible outcome? I'd simply take down one more lousy strand of Christmas lights. Not-so-good outcome? I'd find myself preaching next weekend from a wheelchair in a body cast. Worst possible outcome? In place of our regular service, our church would be holding my funeral.

2.2 Cause and Effect

Our stories are the result of many different variables. You don't get to choose your parents, your family, or where you're born. During childhood, we had all of our big decisions made for us— where we lived, which school we attended, what we ate, even our bedtime. As we got older, the grownups responsible for us gradually handed us more responsibility, letting us make choices and expecting us to face any consequences.

And that process just continues during adulthood. Part of becoming a mature adult is learning over time to accept responsibility for your choices. You learn that if you drive over the speed limit, you could get a ticket. If you date the wrong person, you could end up heartbroken, struggling to trust again. And if you beer-bong a six-pack of cheap beer in less than twenty minutes, you'll find yourself hugging a toilet as if you just asked it to marry you and it said yes.

On the other hand, if you show up at work on time every day and do your best work, your boss approves and gives you a raise. If you start exercising and you improve your diet, your waist size shrinks and you feel better about yourself. And if you attend class, listen, take notes, and actually study for exams, good grades are not out of your reach.

> **Wisdom is God's navigational tool for helping us make decisions about the life we want to live.**

Every choice you make, both big and small, affects aspects of your life. You either learn to take responsibility for your actions, or you learn to make excuses and find scapegoats. Even when things happen that are beyond your control, even when—no, *especially* when—you make mistakes, you still choose how you respond. Wisdom is God's navigational tool for helping us make decisions about the life we want to live. The tricky part is stopping for a moment and actually using it before we make the wrong decision.

2.3 The Rest of the Story

Certainly I was making a mistake that day I went up on my roof with a huge boot on my foot. After sliding halfway down the roof, I chose to take my story where I wanted it to go. I slowly made my way back over to my ladder, clunked my way down, and hugged my wise little girl. The Christmas lights would just have to wait. (If my next-door neighbor said anything, I'd show him where I kept our ladder and thank him for offering to help.)

Thank God I hit pause and sorted through the story's possible endings.

But there were plenty of times when I didn't, when I spoke without thinking first or acted on impulse or reacted without weighing the consequences. I can't tell you how many times I found myself reaping what I sowed, dealing with the consequences of yet another bad decision. "If only I could go back and do it over! I wish I hadn't done that."

And I know I'm not the only one. As a pastor, I have sat with so many people filled with regret, my heart aching for them as they asked tearfully, "Why did I do that? What was I thinking? I would give *anything* to be able to go back and make a different choice."

One of the best decisions we can make when feeling an impulse or facing a high-stakes dilemma is simply to stop. Take a time-out. Hit pause. Sleep on it. Think it over. Get some godly wisdom from people you trust.

During this interval, visualize what's likely to happen with each of your options. Long before my rooftop escapade, I developed this same habit to help me make the best decisions I can. I try to picture the likely consequences of my options. I take stock of where I am and where I want to go, and then move toward my destination. Even if it seems like I'm moving in baby steps, as long as it's in the right direction, I know I'm getting closer to my goal.

Most of us have good intentions, or at least some kind of

justification for the things we do. And yet so many of us seem surprised when we find ourselves a long way from our destination. As we discussed, the big changes in our lives—both negative and positive—rarely happen without a series of decisions dominoing one into another.

Don't let the simplicity of this little habit of stopping to visualize the likely outcomes fool you; it can help you connect the dots between where you are and where you want to be. You already know where you are (or if you don't, that's another good reason to stop: so you can figure it out), so now you simply visualize where you want to go. Then each time you're presented with a choice, consider the potential outcomes of each possible decision. Which one of them will best move you in the direction of where you want to end up? Which one will lead you closer to God? Treat each choice like it's the next stepping-stone toward your destination. Ask yourself:

1. If I go down this road, what story will I end up telling?
2. Is that what I want my story to be?

Your decisions today, both big and small, determine the direction your life will take tomorrow.

2.4 Stop Signs

Stopping to consider whether our choices will take us in the right direction is important. But sometimes we head in a direction we know is the wrong one, moving farther away from the story we want to tell. When this happens, we need to pause not only to consider the consequences but also to choose to stop traveling in the wrong direction. The word *repent-ance* literally means to change course, to stop walking in one direction and return to God and his path for us.

> Your decisions today, both big and small, determine the direction your life will take tomorrow.

There's a great example of stopping to reconsider a better course of action in the Old Testament. In Exodus 18, Moses knew something had to change or he was going to fall apart trying to manage all the demands on his life. After successfully leading the Israelites out of slavery in Egypt, Moses became responsible for hearing all of the Israelites' problems and handing down judgments. He kept this up, all day every day, until he was spent.

Finally, Moses' father-in-law, Jethro, came to offer him some tough love: "What you are doing is not good. You and these people who come to you will only wear yourselves out. The work is too heavy for you; you cannot handle it alone. Listen now to me and I will give you some advice" (Ex. 18:17–19).

Can you relate? Are you juggling so many chainsaws that it feels impossible to keep going, but also impossible to stop? What keeps you in this situation? What are you doing today that's not good for your story? Do you have some habit, a mindset, an addiction, an attitude, a thought process, something in your life that's hijacking the story you want to tell?

You need the same encouragement Jethro offered to Moses: "May God be with you" (v. 19). He went on to suggest a simple, practical solution. Stop doing it the way you've been doing it and get some help. Jethro told Moses to select a few capable leaders and train them to handle the disputes he had been hearing himself. He described a system that could handle the volume of complaints without overwhelming any of the leaders, essentially a hierarchy in which some people would oversee thousands, some hundreds, some fifties, and some tens. Delegation 101, right?

Instead of Moses taking all of that responsibility upon himself, he could delegate his authority in a way that everyone would still be heard, leaving Moses to deal with only the most complicated and important cases, the ones his managers couldn't handle themselves. If he shared his responsibilities, he could make his load lighter, and everyone would go home satisfied.

Apparently, Moses didn't have to think twice: "Moses listened to his father-in-law and did everything he said" (v. 24). He stopped trying to do everything himself. And that made all the difference. Most of the great stories we have about Moses' exceptional leadership, the things we

> God may call you to abort, abandon, or abolish something, to stop one thing that helps you live the story he wants you to tell.

remember him for, took place *after* he made this one simple, practical change.

Don't miss the importance of Moses' decision. It wasn't that he did more. He did less. The choice to stop doing something not only changed his circumstances but also changed the story Moses would one day tell. The same is true for you. God may call you to abort, abandon, or abolish something, to stop one thing that helps you live the story he wants you to tell.

Many times we must let go of what we've been holding so we can receive what God wants to give us.

2.5 You Don't Know What You're Missing

If you're overwhelmed like Moses was, think about all of the plates you're trying to keep spinning, everything you've made yourself responsible for. Could any of these things hinder your story? For each activity or responsibility, answer these two questions:

1. If I keep doing [blank], what story will I be telling?
2. Is that what I want my story to be?

What's it going to cost you if you don't slow down? One hidden cost might be that you can't know what you're missing if you continue at your current pace. You've grown so accustomed to your habits, lifestyle, and busyness that you've forgotten what it means to truly relax, to be still before God.

People who have too much to do may have reasons for not delegating—a desire for control, a structure that relies too much on them, poor communication skills, lack of management ability. In many cases—maybe even in most cases—they burn out. One morning they wake up and can't get out of bed. They just curl into the fetal position and give up.

Most of us know people—other believers—who one day find themselves angry at God, bitter because they feel defeated, beaten by life. What if that had happened to Moses? "God, these are *your* stupid people! Why do *I* have to do all this by myself? Where are you? Why don't you help? Forget you, God!"

Although the Bible tells us that Moses was a great man of faith, we can also see in the details of his life that he wasn't perfect. What would his story have been if he hadn't applied the wise advice he'd received? Imagine what it might have cost him if he hadn't stopped. In the same way, there's no telling what your bad habit, wrong mindset, or unhealthy patterns could cost you if you don't stop. What seems like an inconsequential decision often ends up snowballing into an avalanche.

2.6 Fast-Forward Your Story

Remember, you can discern the impact of your choices and habits by playing them forward. Direction of action, not good intentions, determines your destination. Where is your story headed right now? What will happen if you continue in this direction?

Let's consider a few examples.

Let's start by thinking about your body and how you treat it. Keep overeating. Continue ignoring your body. Don't stop smoking or drinking excessively, doing whatever you're doing that abuses your body in some way. Play that story forward. What's going to happen?

It could be that you don't walk your daughter down the aisle at her wedding. Because you're dead. Maybe you'll never see your grandkids. Because you're not here anymore. Or let's imagine what it might be like to spend the final twenty years of your life battling health issues because of the decisions you're making right now. Playing your story forward can be a sobering exercise. Sorry to sound so dramatic, but people make bad choices—small ones, every day—that lead to tragic endings like these. Or worse.

Just keep right on looking at porn. You've been pretty careful to keep it secret so far, and you haven't been caught yet. Now play that forward. How long will "just looking" be enough? How long until you're hooking up with some old flame you found on Facebook, and both of you end up destroying your marriages? Or maybe you don't ever do anything more than just look, but one day you come home from work to discover that the person you vowed "till death do us part" has found out what you've been up to. Crushed, devastated, heartbroken, your spouse cries, "Was I not enough for you?"

Keep spending more money than you make. Charge everything you can on credit cards, and when you've hit your limits, just apply for more. Play your story forward. One day when you realize you can't even keep up the minimum payments anymore, try explaining to your kids why they have to quit the activities they love—soccer, dance, piano—because you can't afford them. Tell your family you have to sell the house and everyone has to move into an apartment and change schools because you've run out of options. Just play the story forward.

But there's good news: your story doesn't have to end this way. Just like Moses stopped one thing and dramatically altered his story for the better, you can stop the one thing that will start you on the journey toward a better, God-glorifying story.

2.7 Inside Outside

Even though you can probably come up with several things you need to stop doing, for now pick only one. If you pick five, I can guarantee that you won't be successful at stopping any. Pick just one. As you consider which one, examine both your external and internal habits.

External habits are behaviors that can be observed from the outside: eating unhealthy things, losing your temper and going off on people you love, activities or behaviors that harm yourself or others.

Even more dangerous than the external behaviors is our internal sin nature. That's what gets us into trouble most often. Selfishness, greed, pride, lust. A bad attitude, a critical spirit. Even worrying and negative self-talk. Whatever is going on internally that's not good, you need to stop it. I know, because I've had to stop a few things in my own life.

When I was in college, before I was a follower of Christ, I drank alcohol. Like, a lot of alcohol. Like a whole lot. I would get sloppy drunk with my friends on a regular basis, take my shirt off and start to dance—badly. But then when I gave my life to Christ, drinking was one of the first things I realized I needed to stop. For me, drinking inevitably led to all sorts of other dangerous behaviors and sins. Giving up alcohol was truly a struggle for me, but thankfully, God empowered me to want more than what a six-pack and a few shots (okay, a lot of shots) could provide. So I stopped. It wasn't easy at first, but the more I practiced leaving alcohol behind, the more I headed in my new divine direction.

During that same time, while I was still single and partying, I was also sexually active. But I realized that external behavior was not helping me tell the story I really wanted to tell. It's not that I wanted pure relationships; what I actually wanted was just one pure, holy relationship with one woman for the rest of my life. So after a lot of prayer and wrestling with God, with his help I stopped having sex before marriage.

Then after Amy and I met and fell in love, we agreed to keep our relationship pure by waiting until we were married to have sex. Even though it wasn't easy (to say the least), it was unquestionably worth it. Now we can share with our children and our church family the truth about our story and our choices, which is helping them make choices that will tell the stories they want to tell, stories they can be proud of.

I also used to throw temper tantrums. I had a really short fuse, often flying off the handle when something upset me. With God's help through trusted friends, over time I've learned to count to ten before I react. These days, although I can still be really intense—at least, according to the people who work with me—I don't struggle with my temper like I used to, which empowers me to be a better parent, husband, and pastor.

Not so long ago, my family pointed out another thing I needed to stop doing. Both Amy and my kids told me, "It seems like you're always on your phone." At first, I tried to justify it. "But this thing I'm texting about is really important!" It didn't take me long to recognize that they were right. After detoxing from my phone addiction, I managed to stop bringing my phone to meals. I gradually learned to stop being a slave to my phone. I want my story to be, "Dad was always engaged with us," not, "Craig always replied to every text in five minutes or less."

Because which one actually matters?

2.8 Quitting Time

I've given you a few examples from my life. Now it's your turn. What does God want you to want? And based on what God wants you to want, what does God want you to stop?

Remember: focus on just one thing for now. Each example I've given you was one thing I worked on for a considerable amount of time—weeks, months, sometimes years.

Let's consider a few common things people struggle with to help you think through which things you might need to stop.

SOCIAL MEDIA

Is your devotion to social media taking over your life? One day a few months ago, my sixteen-year-old daughter invited several of her friends over to our house to hang out. I walked through the living room and saw them all sitting together on the couch, all looking down at their phones! They might as well have not even been in the same state with each other.

How much time have you spent on Pinterest in the past week? And did some picture of cake you found on there change your life? Was it worth the time you invested tapping around? Did you post a recipe that changed the world? Are people writing you letters to thank you for how much that lampshade you glued lace on has meant to their family? Look up from that screen! You might very likely find a few faces right there in the room with you, people who love you, who are desperate for you to connect with them.

THE NEED FOR CONTROL

Are you trying to control everybody and everything in your life? Take a deep breath and have an honest look around you. Are you driving your kids away? Are you constantly making your spouse crazy? What you are doing is not good. You need to stop being a control freak.

Are you critical of everything? Are you judgmental? Do you carefully evaluate everything around you, constantly picking out the things you don't like? (Is that what you've been doing since the first page of this book?) So let me ask you, has it helped? Is the world a better place because you're committed to picking things apart? Ask yourself, "Is what I'm doing good?" If it's not, stop. And who knows? If you can stop judging everything, you just might be surprised at how much more you start enjoying your life and the people in it.

UNHEALTHY HABITS

Do you smoke cigarettes? Cigars? Cigarillos? Weed? Crayons? Cardboard? Whatever you can find that will roll? If that's what you're into, that's not good! It's not helping you. You need to stop.

Do you enjoy a drink now and then? Maybe a lot more "now" than "then" lately? Have you been lying to others about it? Have you been lying to yourself? You need to take responsibility for your choices and stop.

Look at the people you have around you, your friends and acquaintances. Are they helping you make a great story? Are they loving you, encouraging you to live a life that honors God, that makes a difference? Or are they just dragging you down with them?

You may need to stop hanging out with them. Are you constantly eating things you know are bad for you, fast food and junk food?

If you're watching questionable movies and TV shows and listening to music that you know doesn't honor God, you need to stop.

If you've been neglecting your family for other things, you might seek counseling, find a different job, take some time off, or do whatever will help you stop.

If you've been blaming God for something bad that happened in your life, seek God in his Word. Talk to your pastor. Pray about finding a way to stop blaming the one you need most. If you're holding on to some hurt feelings because somebody did you wrong, ask God to help you forgive them so you can stop being held hostage by bitterness. But do *something* to move from where you're stalled.

What are you doing that's not good for you? What do you need to stop so that you can tell the story God wants you to tell? What's the next decision you need to make to change the direction of your life? What is it that you need to stop so that you can move forward in the story you want to live? Pick one thing you know you need to stop doing in order to change your story's direction. Write it down on a piece of paper.

2.9 The End in Sight

The writer to the Hebrews said, "Since we have so great a cloud of witnesses surrounding us, let us also lay aside every encumbrance and the sin which so easily entangles us, and let us run with endurance the race that is set before us, fixing our eyes on Jesus, the author and perfecter of faith, who for the joy set before Him endured the cross, despising the shame, and has sat down at the right hand of the throne of God" (Heb. 12:1–2 NASB).

What is the one thing that's restricting you, hindering the story you want to tell? Lay it aside. One translation says "throw it off."

This is a long race we're in. You have to pace yourself. You can see the trail marked out ahead of you. You know what's wrong. You know what you're doing that's not good. Seek help. Read a book. Seek God in a fast. Join a small group. Do whatever you need to do to stop it. And if that doesn't help, try something else.

Fix your eyes on Jesus. Give him the opportunity to write your story. Don't be embarrassed to ask him for help. He wants to perfect your faith. This isn't behavior modification; anyone can do that. What you need is spiritual transformation. You need to get clear of the clutter so you can hear from God. Then you need to listen. He'll show you the things that are hindering your story.

Maybe you recognize something you've been doing that's not good, and you've already tried to stop, but you found you couldn't do it on your own. It's true that *you* can't, especially on your own. But I'm here to tell you that by the power of Christ, you can stop anything that he calls you to stop. If you follow Christ, then the same Spirit who raised him from the dead dwells within you!

And he will give you the power to stop.

3 Stay

I have more care to stay than will to go.

—WILLIAM SHAKESPEARE

*B*usy shoppers milled around him, some pushing carts, others holding small plastic baskets. Canned music played overhead, and somewhere nearby a child cried. He stood in the aisle with all the greeting cards, and the variety overwhelmed him. He was looking for something serious but not too sappy, maybe lighthearted but not silly. With these dozens—if not hundreds—of cards, why was it so hard to find just one that said something close to what he wanted to say?

He hated picking out anniversary cards for this very reason. They weren't newlyweds anymore—far from it. But they weren't *empty nesters ready to retire either. Something sexy and flirty didn't seem right, although he didn't mind either one after the kids were in bed and it was just the two of them. But it had taken them months to get back to the point where they were comfortable being alone together. He thought back over the past year and wondered if they had made the right decision, and reflected on what the perfect card might say.*

"Hey, honey—happy anniversary. We made it another year. I wasn't sure we were going to pull through what happened last summer, but I'm so grateful you were willing to stay and work it out. It would've been so much easier for you to blame me and just leave. I know a lot of wives would assume divorce was the only solution. I know I've said it a million times now, but I'm so sorry I hurt you. We don't need to rehash the past, but I want you to know how much I love you. How much I appreciate your willingness to talk things out and cry together, pray together. How much your forgiveness means to me. No one has ever loved me the way you do. Thank you for staying, for not giving up on our marriage and our family. I love you. Happy anniversary."

He casually wiped the tears away and looked around to see if anyone noticed, as if anyone could even know what he was thinking and feeling right then. An older lady a few feet away laughed out loud at the card she was holding and then glanced up at him as if waiting for him to laugh too.

"It's silly," she said to him, or maybe to no one in particular, "but I think my husband will like it." She leaned toward him, so he realized she must be talking to him after all. "It's our anniversary tomorrow. Forty-eight years—can you believe it?"

He smiled and nodded. "My wife and I are celebrating an anni-versary too."

"Good for you," she said. "You didn't ask, but I'm going to tell you the secret to a good marriage."

He stepped closer and noticed the sparkle in her eyes.

"Mostly, just being willing to stick it out," she said. "It's choosing to stay when it would be easier to go."

He nodded in agreement as she walked around the corner to the next aisle. He wondered if she was an angel or just some crazy old lady. It didn't matter. He grinned, grabbed a blank card with plenty of space to write his own anniversary message, and headed toward the checkout line.

3.1 Quitting Time

It's only by the grace of God that I've been a pastor for more than half my life now. When I first decided to completely follow Christ, I was still in college, working toward a business degree. As soon as I knew I wanted to dedicate the rest of my life to serving God as a pastor, I started looking for opportunities to serve.

Even though I had no ministry background, my home church was willing to hire me to start a ministry to single adults. I faced a huge learning curve, making more than my share of rookie mistakes. And then, at a Friday night singles event, it happened. Everyone realized that in only a few short months, I had turned things around—only it was in the wrong direction! What had started as a strong group of around a hundred people had plummeted to only four or five—and Amy and I were two of them!

After that Friday night disaster, it didn't take long for one of the church board members to call me in for a meeting. He said, "Listen, Craig, we've been talking about it, and we're really not sure this is for you. Maybe you should consider doing something else with your life." I knew things weren't going well, but I was stunned.

Devastated, I went straight home to tell Amy what had happened. I couldn't contain my emotion. When God had opened this ministry door, I thought he was showing me what I was supposed to do with my life. But after such a failure, I couldn't help thinking I must have been wrong. Maybe I had missed God's direction. Maybe I needed to find a job in a different field. I listed all the reasons I wasn't cut out for ministry: I didn't have any background in it, I was too young, I hadn't been a believer very long—my list of nonqualifications could have filled several pages of a worthless resume.

Amy, on the other hand, reminded me of all the ways that we felt God had already confirmed we were right where he wanted us. Perhaps most important, she encouraged me not to decide anything until I could meet with my pastor, Nick Harris. When I went to see Pastor Nick a few days later, he had already heard about the board's discussions. Even so, he asked me to share exactly what had happened, and he listened patiently to my side of the story.

When I finished talking, my pastor sat there behind his desk for several minutes, studying me, collecting his thoughts. When he finally spoke, he chose his words carefully. "Craig, I think I understand where the board is coming from. And let's just be honest here: they have some valid concerns." I knew he was right, and I suspected he was about to offer me help finding a position elsewhere.

"However," he continued before I could say anything, "here's something *else* you can be sure of: the more God wants to use you, the more likely you'll be tempted to quit. And I think that's exactly what's happening here, Craig. I see real potential in you. You came here to ask for my advice. Well, here it is: don't you dare quit. You stay the course."

I was shocked. And grateful. Sure, Pastor Nick's words were kind and encouraging. But more than that, they carried an authority that seemed to come from some deeper place, from some profound wisdom that I wanted to have too. It was as if God was speaking through him.

And despite hearing the message clearly, I knew it wouldn't be easy to stick it out. It wouldn't even be like starting from zero. I was going to have to claw my way back up from several stories below basement level. But I decided to stay in ministry, even though it would have been easier to walk away.

With my pastor's support, the board agreed to give me another chance to prove myself. And here we are twenty-six years later, and I'm sharing this in a book that you're reading. Because I decided to stay, my story—or should I say, my story in God's hands—has been infinitely better than I ever could have written on my own.

3.2 Staying Power

I've thought many times about how different my life would be if I had given up back then. My story could've become something like, "Yeah, I used to think I was supposed to be a pastor, but I gave it a shot and things didn't work out. That's just how it goes." It wasn't that being something other than a pastor would have been a step down; it was simply that being anything other than a pastor would mean I wasn't following the story God wanted to write in my life. Even though I was tempted to quit full-time ministry, deep down I knew that being a minister was the direction my story should go. It just didn't feel the way I wanted it to feel in that moment.

I'm certain you'll have to wrestle with occasional challenges in different seasons of your life: a job you don't think you can stand for even one more day, a relationship that has suddenly taken a turn for the worse, a dream you've been working on that hasn't materialized yet, a move that hasn't lived up to your expectations. When these things happen, it's only natural to ponder those huge, life-altering decisions:

- Should I take my chances, quit this job, and look for something else?
- I wonder if this relationship has run its course. Could it be time for me to move on?
- It doesn't look like this business is ever going to catch on. Maybe I should cut my losses before things get any worse.

In each of these examples—and with most major life choices—

you've arrived at a fork in the road, and it's time to decide: should I stay the course, or should I walk away?

There are plenty of times when you should just walk away. Sometimes the best thing you can do is to allow this chapter of your life to end so you can start a new one. Before you decide, you really need to ask yourself, "Am I choosing to give up because it's the right thing, or just because it seems like leaving would be easier?"

But it may be that the best and most rewarding decision you can make is to stay the course, even when it would be so much simpler to turn and walk away.

3.3 Ruth or Dare

Sticking it out is never easy. If you weren't conflicted or facing some kind of adversity, you probably wouldn't be tempted to make a big change. Many times—maybe most of the time—it won't seem logical to stay. Sometimes the best decisions we make go against conventional wisdom or

> It may be that the best and most rewarding decision you can make is to stay the course, even when it would be so much simpler to turn and walk away.

trends. That's why it's so important to listen to what *God* tells you, not everyone else.

The Old Testament tells us a great story about this very dilemma in the book of Ruth, where we meet a woman named Naomi and her two daughters-in-law, Orpah and Ruth. Their story begins with tragedy. First, Naomi's husband died during a famine.

But she had two sons, who both married Moabite women, Orpah and Ruth. Then about ten years later, tragedy struck again; both of Naomi's sons died. That left all three women without husbands.

At that time, a widow without children was pretty much without hope or opportunity. Society wasn't set up for women to work, so a woman was dependent on her husband for income, and then on her children if her husband died. It wasn't like Naomi could just try to make ends meet with a job at a coffee shop. By no fault of her own, Naomi's only option was to become a beggar, a position in society even lower than a slave.

Because Naomi understood the grim reality of their situation, she graciously encouraged her daughters-in-law to return home. "You've both been so good to my sons and to me. You're great girls. You should go home to your families. It will be easier for you there, and besides, you're both still young enough to find husbands." After some convincing, Orpah realized what Naomi was saying was right, so she went home. While it was the easy thing to do, certainly there was no shame in it. And besides, it clearly made the most sense.

But Ruth saw things differently. Even though it would have been much, much easier for her to go, she chose instead to stay, to stick by her mother-in-law despite the uncertainty of the future. Naomi tried to talk her out of it, telling her sweetly, "Look, your sister-in-law is going back to her people and her gods. Go back with her" (Ruth 1:15).

But Ruth replied, "Don't urge me to leave you or to turn back from you. Where you go I will go, and where you stay I will stay. Your people will be my people and your God my God" (v. 16).

When Ruth tells Naomi she's going to stay with her, it's serious; she's committing to this life. She's saying, "We're family, and even though I know it's going to be hard, family sticks together." But the next thing she says is actually much more powerful to me. She says, "I'm not going back to the gods I had before. I'm choosing *your* God, Naomi, the one true God. I'm not just committing to you; I'm committing to him."

It would be difficult to overemphasize just what a big deal this decision was, how costly it was for Ruth. Her decision was to become a beggar, less than a slave, right alongside Naomi. Can you imagine choosing that life on purpose? And yet that's exactly what Ruth did. She had grown to love and trust Naomi. But more than that, she chose to place her trust in God.

As she adjusted to her new life in a strange land, Ruth went out into the fields after the harvest to pick up leftover grain. (This was according to a law that God had put in place during the time of Moses, telling landowners to allow the poor to gather whatever reasonable amount of grain they could carry.) If the harvesters left any behind, Ruth would have grain that she and Naomi could use to make bread. But if the workers were really thorough during the harvest, Ruth might go home empty handed, and they'd go hungry.

One day, the rich man who owned the fields where Ruth was going saw her, and he felt compassion for her. This guy's name was Boaz, and when he learned what Ruth was up to, he gave her his permission to gather there and even to drink from his well when she was thirsty. Then he instructed his workers not to bother her and to leave behind extra grain so she'd have enough.

It wouldn't have been unheard of during that time for men to take advantage of a woman in Ruth's lowly circumstances, so Boaz even went so far as to warn his men, "Don't you dare lay a hand on her."

All of this prompts the question, Why would a rich landowner like Boaz show such compassion to some no-name foreign girl like Ruth? Because he had heard her story, the story her life was telling about loyalty and love. Just look what he says to her in Ruth 2:11–12: "I've been told all about what you have done for your mother-in-law since the death of your husband—how you left your father and mother and your homeland and came to live with a people you did not know before. May the LORD repay you for what you have done. May you be richly rewarded by the LORD, the God of Israel, under whose wings you have come to take refuge."

Boaz had heard how Ruth selflessly decided to stay with Naomi when it would have been easier for her to go. And not only did he compliment her for her loyalty to Naomi, he also arranged for her life to be a little easier, then topped that off with a blessing. You have to understand, in their culture this was much more than simply a nice gesture; blessings tended to be reserved for family members—in particular, sons who were heirs. For Boaz to offer Ruth such a blessing was truly unprecedented.

Neither Boaz nor Ruth imagined just how big that blessing would become. Through a series of unusual events, Boaz—the kind, generous, wealthy, respected landowner—ended up marrying Ruth. After they married, Ruth and Boaz had a son. Even after Ruth died, her story still wasn't over. If you trace the lineage of Jesus, you'll see that he came from her bloodline. And certainly this influenced the fact that Ruth had a book of the Bible named after her—one of only two women to have that distinction.

Everything in Ruth's life changed. Why? Because she decided to stay when it would have been easier to go. It's also important for us to recognize that Ruth didn't stay because she thought there might be something in it for her. She wasn't just hoping God would somehow bless her. No, she stayed because she believed it was right, and that's why God blessed her.

3.4 Should I Stay?

If you haven't already, you will someday find yourself at a crossroads, a place where you have to make a difficult decision about your life's direction. "Should I stay the course when it would be easier to go another way?"

Or maybe a better question you should ask is this: What does God want you to want?

Think about that for a minute. What is the one big thing you know God wants you to pursue? Does he want you to spend more time with your family? Maybe he wants you to spend more time developing your family spiritually. Maybe he wants you to work more to develop *yourself* spiritually because, to be honest, you haven't been growing as a follower of Jesus, a genuine disciple. It may be that God wants you to stop pursuing your own dreams, to surrender something to him that means a lot to you. Maybe he wants you to stop living for things that don't matter. Even if what you're thinking of isn't one of these things, I'd be willing to bet you have some idea what God wants you to want.

In the light of knowing what God wants you to want, where does he want you to stay? In what area of your life does God want you to stay the course so you can tell the story he wants you to tell? Even though it might be easier to walk away, is there some situation where God wants you to stay? Take a moment to jot it down.

As you consider these questions, let me share about another time in my life when I was not only tempted to quit, I actually did quit. My senior year of high school, I was playing in the semifinals of the state tennis championships against a guy who was undefeated. My opponent was favored to win the tournament, so a college scout from one of the top-ranked NAIA schools in the country had come to watch him play. State semifinals were a big deal, so I really played my guts out, just giving everything I had. And lo and behold, I wiped the court with my previously undefeated opponent.

When I walked off the court, the recruiter walked right past him, straight to me, and offered me a full, four-year tennis scholarship to this awesome university! A little while after he left, I played my next match, in the finals, against a guy I had beaten just two weeks before. And he destroyed me. I mean, I probably played the worst match I've ever played.

Nevertheless, I started college the following year as a jubilant freshman with a full scholarship. I should have been terrified, because I was totally, hopelessly outclassed. All the other guys on our team had been recruited *internationally*. They were all from

Australia, every one of them phenomenal. The only reason they kept me on the team was because I was the only player with a car! I was the transportation.

That first year, our team was regularly ranked third or fourth in the *nation*. There were six guys on our team, and I was dead last, much worse than all the other guys. While my low average wasn't sinking our team's ranking, it was clearly lowering morale. About halfway through our season, my teammates' records were something like 16-0, 15-1, or 14-2. And then there was mine: 2-14. And not because I had won two matches. Oh, no! It was because one of the guys I was supposed to play defaulted. He didn't show up!

After a series of frustrating losses, I finally allowed my emotions to get the best of me. During this particular home match, as usual all five of my teammates won easily. And as usual, I lost. But I didn't just lose. I lost 6-0, 6-0! In that moment, I felt strongly that I needed to express my accumulated frustration and disappointment. So I did what any God-fearing person would do: I took out both of my rackets and smashed them.

But that's only the tip of the iceberg. (I'm not proud of these things, so please don't judge me too harshly.) As I was destroying my equipment, I didn't just smash my rackets. I also released a torrent of swear words that would've made demons blush. And then, just to be sure I had fully made the point that I was less mature than a three-year-old, I left that pile of racket carcasses right where I had shattered them, stomped over to our coach, and declared loudly enough for everyone within earshot to hear, "I quit! I'm done! Go ahead—replace me!"

I stormed across the campus, back to my dorm room, and crashed facedown onto my bed. I just couldn't take the disgrace anymore. I didn't care if I never saw any of those people again. (After that display, I really hoped I wouldn't.) Unknown to me at the time, one of my fraternity brothers had witnessed my meltdown. As I was leaving the court, he scrambled to a phone, called my high school tennis coach, and told him what had just happened. As soon as my old coach hung up, he grabbed his keys and hopped into his car. Then he drove—*an hour and a half*—to my college.

I hadn't showered, hadn't changed clothes. I was still locked in my room, stewing and pacing, when there was a knock at the door. I charged over to answer it, furious. There he stood, my high school tennis coach, Ken Ellinger. My jaw dropped open. Words failed me. I thought the world of him. And now here he was standing in my doorway.

He put his hand on my chest, gently pushed me back into my room, and closed the door behind him. He pointed at the bed and said quietly, "Sit down, son."

Of course I was too shocked to do anything else.

He wasn't angry, not condescending or mean. He was assertive, insistent, authoritative. Ken said, "Groeschel, you're not a quitter. Listen to me. You are not a quitter. Do you hear what I'm saying to you? You are not a quitter. You are not a quitter."

He didn't berate me or insult me. He didn't say things like, "What's wrong with you?" or, "You should be ashamed of yourself!" or, "Aw, I heard what happened. I'm so sorry!"

He simply laid out for me how things were going to be. He

inspired me, painting a picture of my future with his words. "I forbid you to quit. I didn't invest all that time in you for you to quit. You are not a quitter. You're a finisher. Now you get your butt back out to that court. You apologize to your coach and to your team and to any people who still happen to be there. And you finish what we started. You finish what *you* started. Do you understand me?"

I nodded obediently. "Yes, sir." I mean, what was I supposed to do?

And then I did exactly what he told me to do. I rubbed my bleary eyes, left him there in my dorm room, and I went out looking for my coach. He seemed startled to see me come walking back. Then before he had the chance to stop me, I just started talking. "I'm sorry. I'm an idiot. I'm sorry. If you'd let me have another chance, I promise I'll work harder than anybody on the team. I'll work harder than anybody ever has. I'm so sorry. I'll do anything you say. I'll never do anything like that again. Again, please just let me say, I am *so* sorry."

You are not a quitter. You're a finisher.

I had already quit. I had already walked away. It would have been the easiest thing in the world simply to never go back. The hardest thing in the world was to stay. But staying was absolutely the right thing to do.

My college coach graciously gave me another shot. (Maybe it's partly because he didn't have another player to replace me.) In the past, I'd cut corners in practice. Instead of giving a hundred percent, I might have given ninety percent. Not anymore. I arrived early and stayed late. I did extra drills on days that were supposed to be off days. I worked as hard as I could. And then, after a long hard slog, less than two years later I went undefeated during our regular season. In my senior year, I was humbled to be named the top athlete at the entire university. They were actually proud to have me!

That's not the best part of the story. More important to me is that God used an incredible man, my high school tennis coach, to plant within me one more simple truth: sometimes it's better to stay. I am not a quitter. With the help of my God, I am a finisher.

What about you? Is God showing you some area of your life where he wants you to stay?

3.5 Finishing Strong

One day you're going to come to a fork in the road. And this new direction may look like the perfect route to take. But no matter how appealing it is, God may lead you to stay the course instead.

Maybe you're in college right now. You've been thinking, *I'm not going to make it. It's too expensive. It's too much work. This is just too hard.* A lot of people would just walk away. That may even be the right thing for you to do, as long as you're sure that's the way God's leading you. But if God is speaking to you—if you're hearing that still, small voice telling you, "You are not a quitter. You're a finisher!"—then put your blinders on.

Get a second job. Get off that unrealistic four-year college plan you've been beating yourself up with, commit to a seven-and-a-half year plan instead, and remain faithful. Semester after semester, just keep plowing away, one class here, two classes there, a summer class over here. Then one day, you'll wake up and realize you have a degree. Your story will be, "You know, it wasn't easy, but today I have a job I wouldn't have been able to get if I hadn't hung in there. I'm not a quitter. I'm a finisher."

Maybe something's happened at your church that you aren't happy about. Maybe someone did something really un-Christlike that challenged your faith. And now you're thinking, *Christians? Really? Whatever! They're a bunch of hypocrites. Forget them!* Someone once said that church would be great if it weren't for the people. The problem is that the church *is* people, and people are imperfect. And imperfect people can make it hard to stay.

But what does God want? Maybe he wants your story to be, "Someone at my church hurt me. Pretty badly, actually. But with God's help, I was able to do for them what Christ did for me: I forgave them. We worked through our differences. That was ten years ago. Today we're at a place spiritually that I didn't even know was possible. Now we don't just go to church, we *are* the church. Together we're making a difference in this world. It would have been so much easier just to go. But today my life is different because I stayed."

Maybe what you're dealing with is even more serious. Maybe you've been trying to come to terms with God. Something happened that you couldn't understand, something you didn't like. And ever since, you've been crying out to God, "Couldn't you have stopped this? Why did you let this happen? If you're going to allow things like this, I don't need you." Your story could be that you walked away from God, just like many people before you.

Or your story might be that you decided to stay with God. You chose to accept that God will never leave you nor forsake you, so you stayed. You chose to trust him and keep talking to him. "I don't understand this, God. It doesn't make sense to me. But I also know I'm not you. I know your ways are higher than my ways. I choose to believe in you even during those times when I can't feel your presence. Still I know you're there."

After some time has passed, maybe you'll be looking back, reflecting on your story, and you'll realize that even though you didn't know it at the time, God was using that very thing that you hated to rewire you, to change you, to transform your life. You perhaps didn't think it was possible, but you've indeed changed in an important way. What the enemy intended for evil, God somehow used for good. Maybe your story will be that you learned to know God and his faithfulness in a way that you never had before. Maybe your story will be that you chose to live for him and his glory in a way you never thought was possible. And all because you decided to stay with God.

Maybe you've already been remaining faithful. Maybe you've been doing that for a long time. You've stayed in the same boring job, and you feel like a failure. You've stayed raising your kids, but you still feel like a failure. You've been stuck in the same boring marriage, and you feel like a twenty-year failure.

But sometimes the greatest act of faith is faithfulness, staying where you're planted. From where you're standing in your field, picking up leftover grain, you may not be able to see your Boaz yet. But "let us not grow weary of doing good, for in due season we will reap, if we do not give up" (Gal. 6:9 ESV).

One of my favorite stories about staying comes from one of my best friends, Bobby Gruenewald. Bobby started and sold two technology companies before he ever graduated from college. Obviously this guy is crazy smart.

Bobby started volunteering for the church in his midtwenties, and we eventually hired him. Although his contribution to the church was extraordinary, he didn't feel like he was making a difference. So Bobby considered quitting and going back into business.

Truthfully, it would have been easier for him. As a pastor, he still had a lot to learn. Business is second nature to him. But by the grace of God, he decided to stay. And among his many important contributions, Bobby came up with the YouVersion Bible App, an idea that has done more for Bible distribution than any idea since the printing press.

> If you are tempted to walk away, make sure to seek God, because you never know what he might do if you have the courage to stay.

So if you are tempted to walk away, make sure to seek God, because you never know what he might do if you have the courage to stay.

Don't give up.

Don't. Give. Up.

Listen to what God is telling you he wants you to do.

Sometimes the right decision is to stay.

Go

*Do not go where the path may
lead, go instead where there is
no path and leave a trail.*

—RALPH WALDO EMERSON

*S*he sealed the last box with packing tape and slumped to the
floor, leaning back against the wall to rest for a moment. Late
afternoon sunlight diffused through the second-floor window,
making her notice the thin layer of dust on the sill. She couldn't
remember ever feeling this exhausted, not even during her resi-
dency, when sleepless forty-eight-hour shifts were the norm. There
was still so much to do: boxes to ship, furniture to be picked up by
friends at their church, final goodbyes to be said.

When she and Scott had decided to move to Haiti more than a year ago, no one seemed to take them seriously. Or they simply couldn't seem to grasp why empty-nesters would walk away from a beautiful house, a thriving pediatric practice, and all the luxuries of one of the most beautiful cities in the country. Why would someone abandon a life they had worked so hard to build, only to go to one of the most impoverished places on earth? A place without reliable electricity? A place where people trusted witch doctors more than modern medicine?

But it had been an easy decision. People had always said about them, "Oh, they have such a heart for missions." But they didn't think about themselves that way. They didn't believe in missions, per se. They simply wanted to help people, especially the poorest in the world, get necessities like clean water, fresh food, and basic health care. She especially enjoyed describing her friend Jesus to the children and seeing their eyes light up. Most of all, she wanted the kids to know that Jesus really loved them, not because she told them so but because they experienced his presence through the simple acts of service her medical missions team would be providing. She felt it was the least they could do to thank God for the countless ways he had blessed them and their family.

She couldn't imagine retiring anyway, sitting idly next to some golf course or some pool somewhere. While that lifestyle didn't particularly bother her—people at country clubs need Jesus too—that wasn't where God was calling them to go.

She heard Scott's voice in the doorway. "You okay, honey?"

She opened her eyes to see her husband standing there, looking at her. She smiled. "Yes. Just finished the last box. Thought I'd celebrate with a little ten-second nap."

He smiled back. "You must be exhausted, baby. I haven't seen you stop moving for days." He leaned against the wall where she was resting and slid down beside her. She raised her head so he could put his arm around her. She laid her head on his shoulder and rested a hand on his chest.

"Are you sure you're okay with all this?" she asked softly.

His smile spread wider. "I thought we agreed we were through talking about this. I'm as sure about it as I've ever been about anything. When God calls you to go somewhere, and then he calls your spouse to the same place . . . Well, it seems pretty obvious to me you'd go together."

She didn't mean to, but she laughed. He had always been able to make her laugh, even when she was trying to be serious—especially then. She lifted her head so she could look into his face. The corners of her eyes flickered, swollen with tears that hadn't fallen yet. "This is going to be hard," she said. "Harder than we think it is. Remember last summer, when we went to—"

"Yep," he interrupted her. "That guy who was there with you? That was me. It's only hard for us. It's easy for God. Besides, he likes us doing hard things. Makes us keep trusting him, keep talking to him, all the time, every day. And that's what we like too. Remember?"

She'd thought she couldn't love this man any more than she already did, and then he went and said something like that. "Yep," she whispered.

4. 1 Who Needs a Bible?

I vividly remember the first real step of faith I took toward God.
I was a sophomore in college, and I wasn't a follower of Christ
yet—far from it. I was vice president of my fraternity chapter that
year, and we were in hot water for our outrageous behavior. We
were in so much trouble that the college considered closing our
chapter.

Our fraternity had already had a couple of meetings to discuss what we could do to appease everybody, but none of us had
any really good ideas. For some time I'd been thinking about
how I could start exploring what God was all about, and suddenly I recognized I had the opportunity to kill two birds with
one stone. So I went to my drinking-buddy fraternity brothers
with a radical proposal. "Listen, guys, I think I know what we
should do. Let's start a Bible study!"

Several of the guys groaned and rolled their eyes. "Are you
smoking weed, Groeschel? No way, man!"

"No, really, I mean it!" I insisted. "Let's just think this through.
We need a really good public relations move, right? What could
improve our image better than starting a Bible study?"

The pushback was immediate. "Nobody's gonna fall for that.
And besides, none of us *wants* to do that. A Bible study? Are you
crazy?"

But being vice president had its advantages. "No, I'm not.
And yes, we *are* going to do it! Tuesday night at seven, starting
this week, we're having our first Bible study."

They weren't happy, but they could tell I wasn't going to

back down. Unfortunately, it was about midday on that Tuesday before it finally occurred to me that I lacked at least one prerequisite for conducting a Bible study: I didn't have a Bible. Today we take for granted that we can just download a free Bible app (like YouVersion, for instance) and have hundreds of versions to choose from. But that day, all I could think was, *Where am I gonna get a Bible by tonight?* I was still mumbling on my way across campus to class when I noticed an older gentleman walking down the sidewalk toward me. He wore a suit and tie and a broad, warm smile. As he approached, our eyes met and he said, "Young man, would you like a free Bible?"

My brain felt like it was overheating. *How could this guy possibly know I need a Bible? Do I look like I need a Bible? Is it really that obvious?* I blurted something along the lines of, "Uh, yes. Yes, please. I need a Bible."

He handed me a tiny paperback book small enough to fit in my pocket and walked away, still smiling. I later learned that this man was a Gideon, a volunteer with Gideons International, an organization that distributes free Bibles all over the world. (If you've ever looked in the drawer of a hotel room dresser, you've probably seen the results of their work.)

Just like that, God provided me with the Bible I needed, even though I didn't know him yet. A few hours later, I strolled into my first-ever Bible study, brand-new Bible in my hand, where seven of my party buddies—none of whom were Christians—were waiting for me. If God could provide me with a Bible so easily, I couldn't wait to see what he had in store for this little gathering.

4.2 Spoiler Alert

That first Bible study of ours was just terrible, at least as far as biblical correctness is concerned. (The next several weren't much better.) Our prayers during those early meetings bordered on sacrilege. We simply didn't know how to pray. I picture God smacking his forehead at some of the things we earnestly petitioned him with. We went boldly before his throne with priceless gems like these:

"Uh, God? This weekend when we go out to party, will you keep us safe? Don't let any of us get killed, all right? Um, okay."

"Hey, God, don't let Spiff's girlfriend be pregnant. Uh, thanks, I guess. That'll do it today."

Yes, these were actual things we prayed. We just didn't know any better.

Having never led a Bible study before, I wasn't really sure about the protocol. We all agreed we should probably at least read some of it. Another guy had brought a Bible with him too, so we decided we'd just take turns reading some out loud, then stop every so often to talk about what we'd just read. I volunteered to read first, so we both opened our Bibles to the beginning.

We read Matthew 1 that first time, but honestly, it was pretty boring, mostly just a long list of improbable names. There was also a kind of cool story about an angel coming to some guy in a dream and telling him not to divorce his pregnant wife. But when we read that their little baby was born and they named him Jesus, we were all like, "Hey! I'll bet this is *the* Jesus!" So we had a pretty good talk about that.

After that first Bible study, I was too excited to wait for next time, so I read on ahead. I read all the way through Matthew. Near the end, they killed Jesus and then buried him, but he came back to life. (I actually knew about that part.) I kept right on reading through Mark, the next gospel, and they killed Jesus again! I remember thinking, *Wow. I didn't know that happened twice.* (I promise this is true.) I was confused, but I pressed on through Luke, and—spoiler alert—it happened again! I thought, *Man, you'd think he'd see this coming after two times.* (I honestly had no idea it was the same story recounted in different ways.) But I was hooked. I couldn't stop. I just kept reading and reading.

I made it to Ephesians that first night. And there, in chapter two, the light came on for me. "It is by grace you have been saved, through faith—and this not from yourselves, it is the gift of God—not by works" (Eph. 2:8–9 NIV 1984).

I surrendered my heart to God the best way I knew how, and I was utterly, totally, completely changed. Can you see how crazy it is that I ended up becoming a Christian? Out of my very mixed (at best) motives, God led me to an encounter with the irresistible truth of his Son.

Just think about that. What happened in that moment? What did it mean?

It means that right now, in *this* moment, as I'm writing this, I can trace these very words you're reading back to one decision I made, one time years ago, to start that Bible study. God met me right where I was. He sent me a Bible through another person who had chosen to obey God's call to give Bibles away. I can't imagine how different my story would have turned out if I hadn't found the faith to go ahead and start that Bible study. From that step of faith, I grew closer to God and the story he wanted to coauthor about my life. Each time I was willing to take a risk, to go somewhere and do something unfamiliar, scary, or uncertain, I learned to trust God more and more. Sometimes the best decision you can make is to go, even when it would be easier just to stay where you are.

4.3 Time to Leave

What about you? Do you sense something new happening in your life? Can you smell change on the wind? Even if you don't feel like anything is different right at this moment, it's always a good idea to keep your heart prepared for change. Because it happens to us all: a new step of faith, a new venture, a new opportunity.

> Sometimes the best decision you can make is to go, even when it would be easier just to stay where you are.

You'll face something new or different, maybe something you didn't see coming. You can't avoid change. Sometimes we're called to stand our ground when change blows in, but many times we need to take a risk. God may have planted a restless desire in you to serve him in some surprising way. Maybe he's given you a burden for a specific group of people or inhabitants of a special place. Maybe he's calling you to go. Follow that hunch and see where it takes you. Take that leap of faith. Embrace the adventure. The best way to make a big jump is to get a good running start.

There's a great story in the Old Testament about Abram and

Sarai (who later are renamed Abraham and Sarah) that I think illustrates this perfectly. In Genesis 12, God speaks to Abram. At the time, Abram was living in a town called Haran, but he was from a city called Ur of the Chaldees. Back in Abram's hometown of Ur, the people worshiped a false moon god named Nannar.

What's significant here is that the one true God chose to reveal himself to Abram, a guy whose only exposure to religion was seeing people worship the moon. God gave Abram a very simple, direct command: walk away from everything you've ever known. "*Leave* your country, your people and your father's household *and go* to the land I will show you" (Gen. 12:1 NIV 1984, emphasis mine).

Leave and go.

It may seem obvious, but to go somewhere else, you have to leave where you are. To go somewhere else, you have to leave what's known, what's comfortable, what's predictable, and what's easy. To step toward your destiny, you might have to step away from your security.

To step toward your destiny, you might have to step away from your security.

Just imagine the kinds of things that must have been going through Abram's mind. *But I've lived here for years, God! I moved here with my dad. This is my home. I like it here. All my friends are here. My house is almost paid for. The schools are great. (I know Sarai and I were never able to have kids, but still.) My best friend lives right down the street from me. Over there is where I get my hair cut. I get my camels groomed just around the corner, and I really trust that guy. I don't want to leave!*

Abram had all of these things he was used to, a life that was comfortable, and here comes God, calling him to go someplace he doesn't know anything about. But God makes Abram a promise. He says, "I will make you into a great nation and I will bless you; I will make your name great, and you will be a blessing. I will bless those who bless you, and whoever curses you I will curse; and all peoples on earth will be blessed through you" (Gen. 12:2–3).

I can imagine Abram talking back to God. "Say what? A great *nation* is going to come from us? Maybe you missed this, God, but uh, we have exactly zero kids. None. We're childless. Sure, we tried for years—and trying was fun! But that never got us any results. Now here I am, seventy-five years old. It's really kind of too late for us. Surely we can't start having kids now. And you're telling me you're going to make us into a whole *nation*?"

I wonder if you've ever made a promise to God like I have.

- "God, if you'll just help me pass this one test, I promise I'll study next time."
- "God, if you'll just let me not get caught, I'll never do this again. I promise."
- "Lord, if you'll just help me finish this big project for work, I promise I'll start sooner next time."

I don't know about you, but most of the promises I've made to God didn't stick. That's because we're not changed by the promises we make to God; we're changed by believing the promises God makes to us.

Let's look in verse 4 at what happens to Abram after God makes his promise: "So Abram left, as the LORD had told him to." Simple as that. Just what God told him to do, Abram did. But what if he hadn't? What if instead Abram had tried to rationalize everything? What might have happened?

Today, because of Old Testament tradition, we sometimes refer to God as "the God of Abraham, Isaac, and Jacob." If Abram hadn't gone, God wouldn't have changed his name to Abraham later when he made a covenant with him (Genesis 17). There wouldn't have been an Isaac. There wouldn't have been a Jacob. We wouldn't know God today as "the God of Abraham" because Abram would have continued serving his old moon god, Nannar.

If Abram hadn't had the faith to obey God, who knows what consequences we might be living with today? Would God eventually have called somebody else instead? Would we refer to him as "the God of Carl, Alex, and Jeff"? We can't know! Thankfully, because Abram had faith in the one true God, we don't have to.

Where is God calling you to venture into new territory?

4.4 A Real Go-Getter

Like our go-getter Abraham, there's going to come a chapter in your life when you sense there's something new, something different that God wants you to do. You'll know there's somewhere you're supposed to go, but you'll have to leave where you are to get there. But if you don't have the faith to go, if you let your fear keep you where you are, you won't know the blessings you're missing.

Here's what I mean by that: if you go, you get to find out what happens. But if you don't, you'll never know what might have been. The difference is that dull, nagging feeling most people call regret.

So here we are again. It's that time to ask yourself, what does God want you to want? If you're going to allow Jesus to be the author of your story, what needs to change? (Remember: direction, not intention, determines destination. You want to live a better story? Then make your choice *today*.) Step back from your circumstances and try looking at your life objectively, from a "big picture" perspective.

Now based on what God wants you to want, what's the very next step of faith you need to take? Even though it might be easier to stay, what will set you in motion?

I'll illustrate by telling you what happened right after I read Ephesians 2 and gave my life to Christ in college. The university I attended was relatively small, and as I said, I was really involved in activities, especially if they had anything to do with partying. A lot of people around campus knew me, and they knew me as that kind of person. So when I first became a Christian, I faced a problem. Even though I knew God had changed me on the inside, I had this reputation.

Then one day I read in Matthew 10:32 that if I acknowledged Jesus before others, he'd acknowledge me before his Father. Then the very next verse said that if I disowned him before others, he'd disown me before his Father. What that said to me was that I really needed to go public with my faith.

Of course, I didn't really *want* to do that. I had seen how my friends mocked other Christians. I knew they'd make fun of me, and I was pretty sure it would cost me a lot of friends. It would have been easier just to leave things the way they were, keep my faith quiet and more personal, but that wouldn't have told the story that God wanted to tell. It was time for me to go public with my faith.

Looking back, I can see now that the way I decided to do it was kind of weird. Back then you could buy all kinds of Christian T-shirts that had cheesy sayings and designs on them. I decided that wearing the name of my Savior Jesus across my chest was a great way to show people that I was different. And boy, did it work! The first day I walked into the crowded cafeteria wearing a Christian T-shirt, people started laughing and pointing. I heard some of the things they were saying:

- "What's up with Groeschel? Is that a joke?"
- "I think it's just some religious thing he's into right now."
- "Yeah, he's going through some Jesus phase. No way it's gonna last."

What happened was pretty much exactly what I thought would happen. People made fun of me, both to my face and behind my back. A lot of my friends wouldn't have anything to do with me anymore. It was embarrassing, and it hurt my feelings.

But it was a great experience for me. (Strangely enough, I had no way of knowing that at the time.) I learned not only to stay committed to God but to develop a sense of humor. And as much as I didn't like being mocked, it prepared me for today. Because when you stand boldly for Jesus, living with criticism is part of the job description. What I experienced years ago helped prepare me to deal with people who dislike what I do today. *That* part of my story strengthened *this* part of my story.

4.5 One and Four

If we fast-forward a few years, past my evangelistic-apparel ministry days, we reach the part of my story I already told you about, when I became the singles pastor at a Methodist church. As you'll recall, after I'd made a few rookie mistakes (okay, maybe more than a few), the board wanted to fire me, but my mentor helped me see that I needed to stay.

Well, the saga continued. I did hang in there, for four more years. And it was every bit as tough as I had expected. But during that time, Amy and I, along with a few others, started an urban ministry. Our church grew and lives were changed as people encountered Jesus through the variety of ministries we extended to our community. We matured in our faith and thanked God that we had stayed when we had been tempted to quit.

And then something unexpected happened. Amy and I both began feeling God stirring us to start a new church. Honestly, that was the absolute craziest thing we could have done. Why would we leave? What we were doing was working! Why would we give that up? We sure didn't want to. We loved where we were. We loved all the people who were coming. We loved the staff we were so blessed to work with.

My pastor even told me I was like a son to him. He pulled me aside one day and told me, "Craig, I'm going to retire in a few years. And when I do, I hope you'll take over the role of senior pastor." That was the greatest compliment I could imagine. This man was like a spiritual father to me. That church had raised us. We were happy. We were comfortable. Things couldn't have been better. The easiest thing in the world would have been to stay. But we really believed God was calling us to go.

So we took our next step with nothing but our faith. We had almost no resources. No chairs. No pulpit. No musical instruments. No offering plates. Our church building was a two-car garage. The only thing we owned was an overhead projector. (If you were born after 1980, you probably don't know what that is. Just think of it as primitive technology.) We had a volunteer, Jerome, who would flip the transparencies (sort of like swiping through pictures on your cell phone) during our worship time.

Jerome had been a drug dealer, but he had recently given that up when he came to Christ. Unfortunately, before Jerome became a Christian, he lost one of his fingers—shot off in a drug deal that went bad. When we started our church, that was all we had: one overhead projector and a four-fingered transparency flipper. I couldn't make this stuff up.

We didn't want to go.

Nobody wants to start something that way.

But God clearly wanted us to go.

4.6 Going, Going, Gone

Where is God calling you to go? Does he want you to lead others spiritually, maybe even start a small group? Maybe you're afraid nobody will come. Maybe you're worried you're not good enough, that you don't know enough to do something like that. You don't even know what you'd talk about. But here's the thing: if you don't try, you will never know what might have happened.

If God is calling you to go, you're going to have to leave where you are. And you sure don't want to miss out on what he's doing. Years from now, you could be looking back on this time in your life and realize, "That was the day my story changed. I wasn't sure what I was doing, but I decided it was what God wanted, and now I'm a part of this great community of believers. I had no idea how different our lives would be."

> **If God is calling you to go, you're going to have to leave where you are.**

What if God's calling you to get involved in some ministry or even to start a new one? As soon as a few months from now, you could find yourself sharing your story:

- "It blows me away how much it has already changed my life to serve inner-city kids."
- "I never would have guessed I had so much to offer the youth at my church."
- "I always felt like I should help repair cars for people in need. I don't even know how it happened, but I started fixing cars for people on weekends, and all of a sudden, a whole bunch of other people pitched in. Now we have a blast together, and we're impacting the lives of the families we're serving."

None of that can happen if you never take the first step.

Is there a book burning inside you? Set that book free. Take the first step. Quit making excuses. Start writing some notes and getting your ideas organized during your lunch breaks. Then on evenings and weekends, or early in the morning before you go to work, fire up your laptop and write.

Is there some job you've always wondered whether you could get, but you've been afraid they might not hire you? Take a step of faith. Call your friend who's good with resumes and offer to take her to dinner if she'll help you get yours together. Then get your foot in the door and ask for an interview. It's true, you might not get it, but you'll never know if you don't try. You have to step out to find out. You have to leave where you are to go to somewhere else.

Do you have a business idea? Look up online how to write a one-page business plan. Then execute it. Years from now, your story could be, "We started with nothing but an idea. But we followed God, and he opened doors and sent us opportunities. Our lives are different today because we stepped out and took the risk when he led us."

Do you have a heart for children in difficult circumstances? Maybe God's calling you to adopt. You could change a child's family tree. Or maybe God's calling you to foster-parent. Then the sky's the limit! You could be reaching into children's lives and changing countless families for years to come.

Whatever it is that you're supposed to go and do, write it down and remind yourself what your heart already knows.

I know what it feels like to start asking yourself questions. "God, I'm afraid. I need details! What's going to happen? What you're asking me to do sounds hard."

And God may answer, "First of all, I don't give my children a spirit of fear, so that's not coming from me. You don't need details. You need faith. And yes, it will be hard. But I didn't call you to an easy life. I called you to a faith-filled life. Put your trust in me. Let me handle the details. I'm pretty good at them."

My wife, Amy, experienced the faithfulness of God a few years back after going forward with a giant step of faith. After spending time with victims of human trafficking, Amy believed she should open up a transition home for women breaking free from abuse and other hardships. But all the advice she received said she shouldn't. She didn't know much about this type of home. The success rate with these women is very low. There are bureaucratic obstacles. And the list of reasons not to go forward grew by the day.

But Amy believed she should take a step of faith. So with no money, no staff, and no house, she invited people who might be interested and shared the vision to help marginalized women. A few days later, someone suggested we visit a house that was for rent. When we walked into the home, we saw a lady named Janet whom we knew from the church. Janet had just remodeled an older home as a rental property, not realizing she was turning it into the perfect home for Amy's ministry. It was in the perfect neighborhood. It had the right number of bedrooms. It had the ideal floor plan. And it was even furnished.

Janet explained that even though she intended to rent the house, she had felt compelled to furnish it, hoping it would help prospective tenants in need. When she heard Amy's vision to serve women, Janet started crying. After some time in prayer, she explained she wanted to donate the house to the ministry. I will never forget the moment she told us. She cried. We cried. Even the repair guy who came in a week later to fix something cried when he heard the story.

When Amy took a step of faith, God met a need in a way that we never could have predicted and wouldn't have even dreamed could happen. Recently we just celebrated another anniversary of The Branch15 house, which has been serving women effectively for the third consecutive year.

You might find yourself in a similar place as Amy. Take that step of faith. Go, even when it would be easier to do nothing. Venture where God is calling you despite what others say. Trust him with the details.

4.7 Faith Forward

Why are those steps of faith so hard, especially at first? Why is it that so many of us don't go, even when we think we're supposed to? Even though we're Christians, and we're seeking God and asking his Spirit to guide us, and we feel something deep inside us that's leading us to go and we earnestly believe it's him—what is it that keeps us from going? I can't speak for you. But for me, when that happens, it's because I'm afraid. I'm insecure. I'm not sure how it's going to work out. I rationalize my way out of it, telling myself I can always do it later.

But those are just excuses. The bottom line is I don't have faith. Here's why that's such a big problem: "Without faith it is impossible to please God, because anyone who comes to him must believe that he exists and that he rewards those who earnestly seek him" (Heb. 11:6). You want to please God. You believe he exists. You've been seeking him. You've asked for his direction. Now you need to apply faith! Take that step, make a change, move outside your comfort zone, risk failing and starting over, but exercise faith in the God who loves you so much he gave his Son for you.

Maybe you're thinking, *I just don't think I have that kind of faith. I for sure don't have the faith to finish something like what he's calling me to.* Then I have great news for you: you don't have to have the faith to *finish*; you only have to have enough faith to start. You need only enough faith for one step: that very first one.

I can promise you, twenty years ago I didn't have the faith to imagine what our church has become. I didn't picture myself writing this book to you. The only thing I had enough faith for was to plug in our overhead projector and turn our four-fingered flipper free. That's all I had the faith to do.

You don't have to have the faith to *finish*; you only have to have enough faith to start. Just take the first step.

Take the first step of faith. Let God do the rest. He wants to anyway. This isn't about you. It's about him. He's the one telling the story. He's the author. He's the perfecter of your faith.

Who knows where he'll take your story if only you'll let him. Here's how you can find out: take that first step, then just keep going. One day, years from now, you'll look back on your life and see the whole story. What's it going to be?

"I felt like God was calling me, but I was afraid, so I did nothing."

Or will your story be, "I sensed God was calling me to do something, and even though it would have been easier to stay, by faith I went"?

You get to choose. Which will you pick? I pray that by faith you'll have the courage to start a discipline that changes the direction of your story. I pray that by faith you will stop something that hinders your story from being what God wants it to be. I pray that by faith you will have the courage to stay the course and be faithful where you've been planted, even when it would be easier to throw in the towel and just walk away. And when the time is right and God calls you, I pray that you will find the faith to go, even when it would be easier to stay.

Just take the first step.

5 Serve

The best way to find yourself is to lose
yourself in the service of others.

—GANDHI

The tropical sun blazed across the hillside. Shari whispered a
quick prayer of thanks for the shady pavilion and the strong
breeze blowing through. It was already afternoon, but many
people were still lined up outside the gate, their faces stoic even
though their dark eyes glimmered with hope. Shari didn't know the
language, although she occasionally caught phrases she recognized
from high school French class. It didn't matter. Her heart didn't
need a translator to understand the desperation communicated by
teen mothers holding three babies apiece or the old men covered
in scabies.

At first Shari felt self-conscious, unsure what she was supposed to do, let alone how to do it. She felt unqualified, ashamed, and unneeded, pouring water from a pitcher she had filled in the janitor's supply closet into tiny Dixie cups.

Then one of the doctors asked her to hold one of the babies, a precious jewel in a frilly pink sundress, while he weighed the girl's mother. The baby smiled at her, blinking. In Shari's arms, the baby's fevered body was limp as a warm dishrag. The doctor had Shari lay her on the baby scale so he could weigh her. The digital readout flashed for a moment, stopping at fourteen pounds, two ounces. Shari gingerly handed the baby back to her mother. They smiled at each other, and the mother nodded and said something Shari could tell was grateful, even though she couldn't understand the words. The mother turned and walked away. Shari glanced over the short intake form to see if she could tell what they had come in for. She felt suddenly faint, as if all the oxygen had escaped from her body in an instant. That tiny baby girl was almost three years old.

Moments like these—and there were many—simultaneously broke Shari's heart and strengthened it. She had been there for only three days, and already she was emotionally exhausted. She wavered between feeling irritated at her friend Tammy for talking her into coming and grateful to her because she knew she would never be able to forget the gentle people here and their profound need for things that Shari had always taken for granted: clean water, nourishing food, basic medical care.

Shari's visit transformed her. She learned firsthand that serving others isn't just a nice thing to do when you have the time but an urgent call from God's own heart. While she knew she would *one day return to this impoverished land, Shari also realized that everyone is in need, that she had plenty of people to serve back home. But her biggest discovery was the paradox that pouring herself out through serving refilled her heart to overflowing. Shari met herself there under the blazing sun.*

5.1 What Your Best Decisions Look Like

Good decisions are often relatively easy to make. But your best decisions are usually much more difficult. They may cause you to struggle between what feels safe and comfortable and what seems risky and uncertain. They may challenge you because you face several good options but struggle to know which one is best. Or they may carry a steeper price than other, easier options. Your best decisions may defy logic or occasionally go against the recommendations of those around you.

However, there's no need to panic. If you're walking closely with God, he will guard your steps and guide you. Even if you stumble into a ditch, take a detour, or get stuck, he can redeem your bad decisions with positive outcomes.

> If you're walking closely with God, he will guard your steps and guide you.

Our God is that good.

Wait a minute, Craig, you might be thinking, *doesn't this undermine what you've been saying throughout this book? If God can work through all my choices, then how do I know when to Start, Stop, Stay, or Go? And does it really matter which one I do?*

Of course it matters, because as we've seen in previous chapters, our decisions have consequences that shape our lives and the lives of those around us. God is consistent. He's for you. He's not a God of confusion but a God of peace (1 Cor. 14:33). Obviously, your best decisions won't go against God's Word or violate his standards.

Your faith-filled, God-honoring decisions have three other things in common. When you're starting a new pursuit, stopping a bad habit, staying in the midst of a storm, or taking a step of faith, you will discover that God is also asking you to:

- serve others,
- connect with community,
- and trust him with the outcome.

While these three actions may be catalysts for growing closer to God and transforming your life the same way Start, Stop, Stay, and Go are, more likely they will emerge as byproducts of your best decisions. Because God calls us to serve people just as Jesus did on earth. God also created us to be relational and to belong to a family of other believers. And no matter what decision we're facing, we will always be required to trust God.

Serving, Connecting, and Trusting are naturally woven into our best decisions. They're intrinsic to who we are as followers of Jesus.

Let's jump in so you can get a clearer picture of each one.

5.2 Good Bones

Serving others does not come naturally to me. I'm a self-centered person. It's not something I'm proud of, but unfortunately, it's true. And whenever I forget that and get caught up in wondering whether I might be Mother Teresa's long lost nephew, my close friend John Bullard is all too happy to remind me of the ugly truth. Of all people, John probably has the best perspective on just how capable I am of putting myself ahead of others.

Several years ago, John and his wife, Jennifer, were considering buying a new home. Since I've always enjoyed looking at houses, John asked me to check it out with him and tell him what I thought. It was nice, just like he had said: a brick, three-bedroom, two-bath house with lots of character. Even better, it had potential, what investors and real estate agents call good bones.

After he had toured me all through the inside, John wanted me to have a quick look at it from the back yard. We strolled out the back door into the middle of the yard, then turned back to take in the house's profile. Specifically, John wanted me to help him examine the roof to see if there were any signs of long-term problems. Then all of a sudden something unexpected happened, something terrible. We heard a low growl, growing steadily louder, paired with the sound of four giant feet galloping toward us.

We spun around just in time to see one of the original hounds of hell bearing down on us. I don't know what kind of dog it was. The raging zombie kind. The Marmaduke meets Cujo kind. Clifford the Big Black Rottweiler. Suddenly John and I were the ones with good bones, two prime cuts home-delivered from the butcher shop.

I'd like to say that I stood my ground and used my God-given talent as a dog whisperer to tame the savage heart of the evil beast. But that's not what happened.

You know how athletes push off to get a strong start? A

swimmer flings himself off the pool's edge to knife into the water. A sprinter explodes off the starting blocks in that opening mad dash. That's what I did. Only what I pushed off of was John.

Now, to hear John tell it, I shoved him to the ground—as a kind of blood sacrifice to the Hound of the Baskervilles—and ran like a five-year-old kid. Reflecting on it now, I can see how he might have interpreted it that way. Certainly I did put both my hands on him, and I did push him toward the dog—accidentally, of course—with my full strength. But for whatever it's worth, I wasn't pushing John *toward* the dog; I was pushing myself *away* from it. John just happened to be in the wrong place at the wrong time. I attribute the fact that he fell more to his weak reflexes than to any malice on my part.

But like I said, I'm selfish.

Because we both simply reacted, neither one of us noticed the chain link fence separating us from the poster dog for the Hunger Games. John landed on his knees, the dog thrashing and slobbering just inches from his face, trying to gnaw its way through the fence.

When either one of us tells this story now, we're prone to exaggerate and enjoy a laugh. But it wasn't that way at the time. And it's just one example of my selfishness, of how quickly I can put myself ahead of others, even people I care about.

5.3 Self-Service

I'm not the only one. All of us can be a bit self-centered. By nature, we are selfish people. Just think about it: you don't have to teach a child to be selfish. Have you ever seen someone sit down with a two-year-old and say, "Sweetie, today I'm going to teach you to be selfish. It won't be easy, but I think you're old enough now to make the jump. So I just want you to hold this ball, and when I ask for it back, you scream as loud as you can, 'Noooo! Miiiine!'"

That's never happened in the history of the world. When push comes to shove (as my friend John can attest), we all look out for number one—me, myself, and mine.

Not only do we have our sinfulness working against us, much of what we see in culture affirms our self-centered tendencies. Some argue that a massive culture shift in 1973 changed everything. You might not have been even close to being born then, but there's a chance your parents experienced this cultural climate change.

I was six at the time, so I'll share what I can recall about this catastrophic switch.

For decades, if you wanted a hamburger at almost any fast food restaurant, it would come however that restaurant prepared burgers. If you didn't like the tomatoes, you could take them off yourself. If they used mayonnaise and you preferred mustard, you were free to scrape off the mayonnaise as best you could and squirt a mustard happy face across the bun.

Perhaps the best-known fast food chain at the time, McDonald's, had a song about one of their burgers. When you ordered a Big Mac, you got "two all-beef patties, special sauce, lettuce, cheese, pickles, onions on a sesame seed bun." If you didn't like the special sauce, the lettuce, the pickles, the onions, or the sesame seed bun (and trying to pick off the cheese was the worst), too bad for you. Why didn't you order a Quarter Pounder instead? The song told you what you were getting. That's how the burger was meant to be eaten.

Until the competition changed the rules.

In a move that rocked the fast food world, Burger King boldly declared that you had choices, options, decisions to make: if you wanted a burger, you could "have it your way!" You read that right. It was crazy! It was your burger, and you could choose what you wanted on it. No mayonnaise? No problem. No pickles? No big deal. No onions? No worries. Extra ketchup? You got it. Burger King even developed a song that, once you heard it, was stuck in your brain forever:

> Hold the pickle, hold the lettuce,
> special orders don't upset us.
> All we ask is that you let us serve you your way.
> Have it your way.
> Have it your way at Burger King.

And the self-centered, consumer-is-king mindset spread like wildfire. There was a new sheriff in town who was always right—you.

You deserve it.

You're worth it.

Get what *you* want.

Enjoy life *your* way.

It's natural in our world to want it our way, and Burger King nailed it, even if it was just a smart marketing move. According to Jesus, life is not all about us, and yet everything in culture tries to tell us that it is. Without realizing what a rabid monster we'd unleashed, we became more obsessed with self than ever before.

One of the quickest ways to forget about God is to be consumed with self. Jesus had pretty direct words for those who wanted to follow him. He said, "Whoever wants to be my disciple must deny themselves and take up their cross and follow me" (Matt. 16:24). We are called not to celebrate, promote, or advance ourselves but to deny ourselves. To pick up our cross, to suffer through not having everything our way, to die to our selfish tendencies.

God wants us to have it *his* way. And we're not talking burgers.

> One of the quickest ways to forget about God is to be consumed with self. We are called not to celebrate, promote, or advance ourselves but to deny ourselves.

5.4 What Would Jesus Eat?

Speaking of food, Jesus made a statement that should make us pause before we order our next burger. "My food," he said, "is to do the will of him who sent me and to finish his work" (John 4:34).

Wow. My food is to serve God. My food is to please him. My food is to complete the assignment that God sent me to do. My food is to do the will of my Father and to finish his work. That's a different kind of nourishment. And one that caused Jesus' disciples to stop and think, just as it does us. At first they were a little confused. Their leader had just finished ministering to a thirsty woman who needed more than water from a well when the disciples realized it had been a while since Jesus had eaten. So his buddies urged him to stop and have a bite so he could keep up his energy.

But Jesus, never one to miss a teaching opportunity, responded, "I have food to eat that you know nothing about" (John 4:32). Now, if your mind is a bit odd like mine, you might imagine the disciples thinking, *You've got food we know nothing about? Have you been hiding some of those new fig and olive Power Bars under your robe? Do you have pockets in there? Sneaking lamb kabobs from the temple concessions? Here we've been starving for hours and you've got some daily bread stuffed in your fanny pack? Why have you been holding out on us, Lord?*

Maybe we're not so weird after all, because the disciples also took the Lord's response literally. "Could someone have brought him food?" they asked (John 4:33). *Maybe when we weren't paying attention, one of the kids in the crowd slipped him another Filet-O-Fish and some fries.*

When the people around us are all saying, "Get all you can! It's all about you," God wants us to contribute rather than to consume. When all of culture says, "Fill yourself," God tells us to fill others. God didn't create us to be takers. He created us to be givers. Rather than focusing on our desires, we are called to focus on the needs of others. Instead of cutting to the front of the line, we are called to wait at the end. God created us to serve.

> When all of culture says, "Fill yourself," God tells us to fill others. God didn't create us to be takers. He created us to be givers.

And while at first it might seem like we aren't getting as much (have you ever noticed how entitled the phrase "my fair share" sounds?), when we give our lives away, we discover a new and counterintuitive truth: When we give our lives, that's when we find them. When we serve others, we're serving God. We are more blessed when we give than when we receive. When we stop obsessing over what we want, only then can we find what we need.

And that kind of spiritual food, that spiritual nourishment, is far better than any burger, even if you can have it your way.

5.5 Your Serve

By the time I was about twenty-five years old, I had been an associate pastor at First United Methodist Church in Oklahoma City for almost five years. During that time, I had the privilege of learning from one of the greatest men of God I've known in my life, Pastor Nick Harris. It's still hard for me to believe that he invited me to start a single adults ministry and gave me the freedom to shape it any way I thought best.

As I explained previously, I made more than my share of mistakes. I was so passionate about promoting everything we did that I frequently got myself into trouble for bringing up singles events every Sunday in church. In our church services, the pastors took turns leading the Apostles' Creed, praying for the offering, and leading the pastoral prayer. And every time it was my turn, before I performed my appointed task, I announced what the single adults would be doing on the upcoming Friday. Every. Single. Time. (No pun intended.)

I had no idea how much my "harmless" announcements were

annoying everyone until someone from the church board called a meeting. Unbeknownst to me, the board had a special assembly to decide whether I'd be a better pizza-delivery guy than a pastor. Thankfully, they agreed to give me another chance, but I was forbidden to announce a singles event during the Sunday service from that day forward.

Since I've always been one to find loopholes, especially when it involves trying to please God more than men, I easily got around this inconvenient little rule. I wasn't supposed to *announce* an event, but they didn't say I couldn't pray about it. (You can probably see where this is going.)

The very next week at church, I was supposed to pray before the offering. Living up to my promise not to announce any more events, I simply led an offering prayer that went something like this:

Dear Heavenly Father, I thank you for your presence in our church today. And God, I give you praise that your people are giving generously to the mission of your amazing church. And I thank you that a very small portion of what is given today will go to support the single adults fellowship happening this coming Friday at seven. Father, I thank you that your Holy Spirit will remind every single adult to bring ten dollars to cover the cost of dinner and bowling. Also I thank you that they will meet by the south door in the lobby and that you will bless that great gathering just as you are blessing this gathering today. As we offer you our tithes and offerings, we love you, God, and we thank you for all your goodness. In Jesus' name, amen.

If you think I'm exaggerating, look up Pastor Nick and ask him. He'll laugh and tell you that's nothing compared with some of my other stunts. And while that story still makes me smile, it reflects a deeper problem that's haunted me my whole life. Feeling fully justified, I was passionate about *my* thing when I should have been passionate about God's thing. The language I used gave me away. To me, it was *my* singles ministry. And we were going to do it my way.

That mindset almost disqualified me from ministry. By God's grace and with help from others, I slowly learned that the ministry was never mine. It was always God's. And the same was true with my life. Because of what Jesus did for me, my life really belongs to him. So to really find meaning and to glorify God in all things, everything had to become more about God and others and less about me. Even when it didn't make sense or feel fair to me. Even when I could find loopholes.

As God was revealing to me a higher calling than the have-it-your-way lifestyle I'd grown to embrace, my pastor taught one of the most memorable messages I've ever heard. Pastor Nick broke down the story about Jesus washing his disciples' feet in a way that deeply affected me. With great emotion, he explained how Jesus was willing to do something for the disciples that they were not willing to do even for each other. Then he read a **"The greatest among you will be your servant" (Matt. 23:11).** few words I'd heard dozens of times before but never heard with my heart until right then: "The greatest among you will be your servant" (Matt. 23:11).

And that's when I made a decision that changed my life,

focus, and ministry. The people in church were not there to fulfill *my* vision. I existed to serve them. *All* of them. Like Jesus, my
food, my nourishment, came from a higher place. Rather than
being concerned only with my hopes, my dreams, my concerns,
I was called to shepherd others. To love them, hurt with them,
pour into them. And that's when I discovered a spiritual banquet
that I didn't realize existed before. My soul's nourishment came
from doing God's will, and these were the blessings I wanted to
share for the rest of my life.

For example, for months, I'd been turning down invitations
to speak at a nearby nursing home. I had spoken at a home a
couple of years earlier, and honestly, it was very frustrating to
me. After working for hours on a message, I delivered it with as
much passion as I could muster to a group of people who couldn't
seem to care less. Two ladies appeared to sleep through the whole
thing. One guy made loud and aggravating noises the entire time.
Another woman kept talking really loudly, even though no one
was listening. Needless to say, my message bombed.

But after hearing Nick's talk about serving, suddenly I
felt moved to say yes to that nursing home invitation. But this
time, instead of preparing a message, I prepared my heart. Very
little changed on the surface. When I visited, some people still
struggled to stay awake. Another person made loud noises.
And sure enough, one woman was talking loudly to no one in
particular.

But instead of being annoyed, I decided to stop and listen.
This wasn't just some old crazy lady. Her name was Marjorie.
Marjorie was a mother to four sons, grandmother to eleven, and

great-grandmother to two. For the next half hour or so, Marjorie graciously shared story after story of her amazing life with me. She grew up during the Great Depression. She met Jesus at a small Assembly of God church after she had gone three days without food. It was the promise of free food that drew her to that church, but the Living Bread she received there changed her life.

One visit wasn't enough to get to know Marjorie. I went back again and again. And each time, I met more people and I stayed longer. I barely talked; I went to listen. Suddenly a small part of my life no longer was about me but was about others. All I had to do was decide to do what God wanted instead of what I wanted.

5.6 Soul Food

As I let go of doing things my way, I discovered more of how God made me with a shepherd's heart. Because we were a downtown church, several times a week homeless people stopped in to ask for help. Since we encountered their needs for food and shelter so often, I learned to refer them to resources and shelters. But one day when someone knocked on the church door, I felt compelled to do more than just refer the older woman I found standing there to someone else.

For some reason, when Lana asked for help, I felt moved to take responsibility for her needs, to serve her directly, and to make sure she experienced the love of Christ during our time together. I recruited some other church members, and we spent several days addressing each critical need. We helped her get cleaned up, gave her some clean, comfortable clothes, and provided some medical attention for her skin infections.

As we served Lana, she became more and more open to talking about spiritual issues. She had sold her body for money, and she carried more guilt than I was comfortable imagining. But the grace of Jesus swept her away. Lana cried out to him for mercy, asking him to make her his disciple.

As a new follower of Jesus, Lana was well liked at the mission. We spent time with her every day, listening, praying, and before long, even laughing. Who knew that someone who had experienced so much hurt could be so funny? After about six weeks, we found someone who would let Lana clean their home, and Lana was earning her own income for the first time in more than three years. By the grace of God, she remained sober, picking up more cleaning jobs and saving enough money to rent her own room in a rundown apartment building. Amy and I were honored to throw her a housewarming party, and I've never known anyone to be as proud of a place as Lana was of hers.

One day when Lana hadn't dropped by for three days in a row, I got nervous. I went to her apartment to check on her, only to realize my worst fears. When she didn't answer her door, I tried the knob and found it unlocked, and went in to discover that Lana was dead. She had suffered a sudden health complication and passed away a couple of days earlier.

On the day I performed Lana's funeral, only four other people (including Amy) showed up. I was sad that day. Not so much for Lana. She had met Jesus. Her suffering was over. Now she was with him. I was sad for me, for us. We had grown to love her and even to need her in a surprising way. Lana gave us a reason to get far out of our comfortable lives. She taught us how to love someone most people wouldn't even touch. She gave us the gift of giving our lives to serve her. And she helped me learn that there is real soul food that satisfies. It's found not in promoting ourselves but in loving others.

> **Serving isn't something we *do*. A servant is who we're called to *be*.**

With all my heart, I thank God for Lana. And I thank him that he allowed me to be a small blessing to her before her life on earth ended. Lana helped grow my faith. Because of her, I realized that serving isn't something we *do*. A servant is who we're called to *be*.

5.7 May I Take Your Order?

It happened again the other day. To be honest, I couldn't even estimate how many times I've had some version of this conversation. I met someone new to our community. Like always, I asked him how his family is adjusting and how they like their new house. Without fail, it's easy to find a way to invite someone new to the community to consider coming to our church. This time, when I brought up church, I found out that this person was already a Christian—a very frustrated one.

Within seconds, he had already told me about seven different churches they had tried since moving here. The conversation went something like this: "We've been church shopping now for almost two months straight, but we just can't find anything that works for us. We liked the worship at one church, but the teaching wasn't deep enough. Then at this other church, we loved the teaching, but the kids' ministry was lame. We tried one church that we thought might be pretty cool, but no one talked to us the whole time we were there." He finished with the line that to me is the death blow. It still breaks my heart every time I hear someone say it: "We just can't find a church that meets our needs."

Now, before I start sounding like critical out-of-touch pastor guy, let me say that I am thrilled that this person and everyone like him wants to find a great church. But the language in this conversation is troubling. For example, "We're church shopping." It sounds like you're out looking for the perfect item of clothing. And the phrase "I can't find a church that meets my needs" is one of the most unbiblical statements any Christian could utter. This is the have-it-your-way mindset. We see ourselves as spiritual consumers. The church is the product. We want to find a product that meets our needs. Before long, this polluted mindset creeps into our theology. Well, since I'm going to church and doing good things, then God should answer my prayers, get me the job I want, help my sports team win the championship, and ensure that my twelve-year-old becomes class secretary. And if any of this doesn't happen the way I want it to, then God failed me. Because remember, everything is all about me. Right?

We forget that we are not made to be spiritual consumers. God has called us to be spiritual contributors. And the church does not exist for us. We are the church, and we exist for the world.

When my mind shifts from being a spiritual consumer—it's all about me, what I want, what I get, what I prefer—to becoming a spiritual contributor, everything changes. I am here to serve God and to love people. I exist to make a difference. God created me to be a blessing to others. My food is to do his will and to finish the work he sent me to do. When we stop just serving because it's the right thing to do and instead start seeing ourselves as servants, that's the moment when we die a bit more to ourselves and Christ is free to live through us to bless others.

> We are not made to be spiritual consumers. God has called us to be spiritual contributors. The church does not exist for us. We are the church, and we exist for the world.

Here's a fun assignment: ask yourself, "Am I more of a consumer or a contributor?" If you are a Christ follower, hopefully you are a valuable part of a life-giving church. When you think about church, how would you rate yourself? Do you drop your kids off in the nursery (without ever serving there), eat a free donut or drink a free cup of coffee, sit in a seat that someone else paid for, enjoy the service, then pick up your kids and go home? If so, you're a consumer.

On the other hand, do you use your gifts to make a difference? Do you invite people to your church? Do you pray faithfully? Do you tithe consistently? And do you serve passionately? Then you're more of a contributor.

Now think about other areas of your life. When was the last time you gave a whole day to help someone in need? If you've done that several times this year, you're contributing. You're using your life to serve others. If you've never done that, or if you haven't given much of yourself in other ways, then you should face up to the truth: you're more of a consumer.

What about your prayers? Are you faithfully praying for

others? Do you ask God to draw those who don't know him into a relationship with him? To heal those who are sick? To help orphans find homes? To bless those who are hassling or hurting you? If you do, then you're contributing with your faith and prayers. If, on the other hand, most of your prayers are focused on yourself—"Bless me, protect me, help me"—then call that what it is: at least in the area of prayer, you're a consumer.

I'm not trying to be harsh. I'm not trying to heap guilt on you. I simply want to encourage you to be honest with yourself. If you are using your life to be a blessing to others today, then later you will relish sharing the stories that God will allow you to tell. But if you're more focused on self-service than on serving others, you're going to end up with many blank pages—lost blessings that you can find only by contributing what God created you to give to the world.

5.8 Your Server Will Be Right with You

So now I invite you to make another decision that could alter your story for the better. Instead of just sometimes doing good things in God's name to help other people, consider making a radical shift in thinking. Rather than seeing service as something you occasionally do, what if you saw yourself as a servant? It's not what you do; it's who you are. If you are a follower of Jesus, you are called to serve him and to serve people in his name.

This is what the church is all about. Sometimes we forget that God never meant for the word *church* to refer to a building. It wasn't until I was in seminary that I learned the history of God's church. For the first couple of centuries, it was incredibly difficult for followers of Jesus to gather. For one thing, their lives were often in danger. They also couldn't own buildings, so finding public places where they could gather was challenging. Then in AD 313, Emperor Constantine declared Christianity a legal religion. For the first time in history, it became safe (at least in some places) for Christians to gather, and for the first time, churches could own buildings.

> Rather than seeing service as something you occasionally do, what if you saw yourself as a servant?

But we have to remember that the church is not a building. The church is the people. That's why I try to remind myself that we don't *go* to church; we *are* the church.

And since we are the church, God wants to use us to serve him. He wants us to use our gifts to strengthen his body. God's Word offers several different lists of spiritual gifts that God gives to people. One of my favorites is in Romans 12. Paul tells the Roman Christians, "In his grace, God has given us *different gifts for doing certain things well*" (Rom. 12:6 NLT, my emphasis). When you think about it, surely there are certain things that just naturally come easy to you. You're wired to do things that other people can't do, and they often admire that you can do those things.

Paul listed seven different gifts: "So if God has given you the ability to *prophesy*, speak out with as much faith as God has given you. If your gift is *serving others*, serve them well. If you are a *teacher*, teach well. If your gift is to *encourage others*, be encouraging. If it is *giving*, give generously. If God has given you *leadership ability,* take the responsibility seriously. And if you have a gift for *showing kindness* to others, do it gladly" (Rom. 12:6–8 NLT, my emphasis).

You likely have at least one of these gifts. One of my seminary professors gave us a memorable way to know which gift we have: Imagine you're at a table in a restaurant with your close friends, about to share some delicious dessert. You see one of your friends is about to stick their fork into their piece of cherry pie. As the fork descends toward the dessert, you notice that the plate is dangerously close to the edge of the table. Before you have time to warn them, they push their fork into the pie and it plops into their lap. What you do next might be a clue to your gift:

- Do you jump up and offer to help? Do you grab a napkin and rush to do whatever you can to clean up the mess? If so, you probably have the spiritual gift of serving.
- Do you look at the poor victim and offer wise advice? "You know, there's really a better way to eat pie. First, you should always keep it half an arm's length from the edge of the table." If you're inclined to lead a Bible study on the subject, you might say, "You know, this incident reminds me of when Jesus gathered with his disciples at a table. In fact, I discovered that the Greek word for table is . . ." If you find yourself offering instructions, you likely have the gift of teaching.
- If you slap your leg, laugh out loud, and exclaim that you've done far dumber things, because you want to make your friend feel better about what happened, you probably have the gift of encouragement.

- If you offer to buy your friend another piece of pie and then offer dessert to everyone else at the table, you can be pretty sure you have the gift of giving. (Or a sweet tooth and a giver's heart.)
- If you start organizing a crew, getting everyone else to follow your detailed instructions to clean things up, you have the gift of leadership.
- And if you look on and say, "Wow, I can't believe you didn't notice how close your plate was to the edge of the table. You should have seen that coming," chances are that you have the gift of prophecy.

No matter what your gift, God has given it to you not just to make your life better but to serve him and others in the church. If you're just going to church and not serving, I can promise you that God wants to do more in you and through you.

I've had the privilege of hearing the stories of several people who grew closer to Christ when they decided to become servants. One is a thirteen-year-old boy named Gavin. After a friend invited Gavin to church, Gavin met the grace of Jesus, surrendered his life to Christ, and was baptized. And even though Gavin wasn't an adult, he started serving. Now every week he worships in one service on the weekend, then serves at the other six. You read that right. A thirteen-year-old boy serves at six services every weekend. Rain or shine, you'll see this fired-up kid welcoming people to church week after week. Serving impacted Gavin's life so much, he asked for permission to get other students involved serving. Now this middle school student has personally recruited and oversees *fifty other students* who serve on our host team. Talk about the gift of leadership! Gavin doesn't just sporadically serve. He is a servant. That's who he is.

Then there's Chris. At the time of this writing, Chris has been sober for 2,983 days. If you were to ask Chris today how many days he's been sober, I can guarantee you he could give you an exact count. Why? Because he's a new creation in Christ. His past is gone. His sins are forgiven. He's clean, sober, and a servant of Christ. So every weekend at church, if you look for Chris, you'll find him replacing trash bags, cleaning the restrooms, picking up trash, and doing everything he can to make the environment pleasant for guests. Someone asked Chris why he does things that most people don't notice. He just smiled and said, "People may not know what I do, but God does, and that's all the reward I need." God changed Chris's life, and now he serves faithfully because he believes that his contribution will help change someone else's life.

Then there's a guy named Dallas. You wouldn't know it if you talked to him, but Dallas fell in with a rough gang when he was just fifteen. By the time he was old enough to drive, Dallas was selling drugs and carrying illegal weapons. By the time he was eighteen, he was sentenced to jail. While Dallas was in prison, Christians started reaching out to him. After he had served his time, Dallas started coming to our church. He passionately opened his heart to Christ, and God's Spirit transformed him. Now, years later, this servant of God meets with thirty high school students every week so that he can share with them the life-changing love of Jesus that reached his heart.

Finally, Adam's story is one of my favorites. Just nine months ago, Adam met Christ when he was working as a bouncer at a bar. Adam told some of our campus leaders what God had done in his heart. Through tears, he said, "When Christ came into my life, a huge weight of sin was lifted off my shoulders, and my heart started working again." Now Adam is one of the most faithful greeters at church. He laughs when he says, "I used to kick people out of bars. Now I welcome them into church." Like the others, Adam doesn't serve just every now and then. He's discovered that *being* a servant is core to his identity in Christ.

God wants you to serve in his church. His church is a body. And every member, every part, is important. So if you are a part of a church but you're not serving, then something God wants accomplished isn't getting done. Because God wants to use everyone—and that includes you—to serve in his church. Because we don't *go* to church; we *are* his church.

God uses his church to feed and nourish his people. God wants you to contribute, not just consume. Your spiritual food is to do the will of God and to finish the work of the one who sent you.

What are some ways you're serving others in your community? In your church? Where—or whom—do you sense God calling you to serve next? On a notepad or in a journal, describe a couple of places or ways you believe God wants you to serve.

5.9 Light Show

We know for certain that we are not made right with God by our good works. We are saved only by grace through faith. And while we're not saved *by* good works, we are saved *for* good works. Jesus instructs us to let our lights shine so that others may see our good deeds and glorify God our Father.

Not only is God calling us to serve *in* his church, he's also calling us to serve *as* his church. Don't miss this important distinction. Yes, we have the honor of serving other believers inside the church, strengthening them to do the work and will of God. But our most important ministry doesn't happen inside God's church. It happens as we *are* the church, shining his light into a dark world desperate for his goodness. Our flame never diminishes when we light the fire of God's love in someone else's life; it only shines brighter. And when we decide that we want to be who God made us to be and to give our gifts away, he gives us even more opportunities to shine—and to be blessed by serving—in return.

> Not only is God calling us to serve *in* his church, he's also calling us to serve *as* his church.

No one intends to be a greedy, selfish person; we all justify our sinful decisions at some point. But the choices we make about serving others help us to take the focus off ourselves and to see the needs of those around us. You get to decide right now what your story will be, both the one you tell and the ones told about you. You can eat the fast food of selfish choices that tastes good in the moment, or you can eat the eternal soul food of serving others and grow closer to God.

My buddy John enjoys telling that story about my pushing him toward the dog, but I sure don't enjoy bringing it up. For most people, the meaningful stories we have to tell involve doing things that matter. How often do you sit around with friends and brag about that time when you cheated to get ahead? Or that moment when you cut corners to get something you wanted? Those aren't exactly things you're likely to put in your highlight reel, are they? Chances are good that when you're accepting some award for job performance, you won't be thanking all the coworkers you stepped on to get promoted.

No, the stories you love reminiscing about are the ones when you helped others, made a difference, lifted someone up. The times when you were a blessing to someone, when you were focused on others, when you served. The decision to serve may not feel natural at times, but when serving becomes our default ambition, we grow closer to God and experience more of who he made us to be.

The moments when you choose to serve others, to put their needs first, determine the kind of stories you tell tomorrow.

6 Connect

*Show me your friends and I will
show you your future.*

—AUTHOR UNKNOWN

F or his wife's sake, Ben tried to remain stoic throughout the
memorial service for his brother-in-law, Jack, a man ten years
his senior whom he had always admired. Jack's deep Christian faith
had sustained him through two years of battling cancer, and now
family and friends had gathered to celebrate Jack's life. Various
people shared testimonials about their relationship with Jack, each
from a different circle of his life—his office, his church, the youth
center where he'd volunteered, on and on. The things that one man
in particular said moved Ben more than anything else.

This man identified himself as a good friend of Jack's, one of six men who gathered for breakfast every Thursday morning for the past eighteen years. They had met at church, and the group had started as a Bible study with more than twice as many guys attending. But as some men left and others joined for a season, then eventually stopped coming, Jack and these other five men came to form a special bond. While they still participated in a Bible study, they also started meeting for breakfast when one of them struggled through the agony of divorce.

Then another member of the "Super Six" admitted his addiction to prescription pain pills, and the other guys joined to help him. The speaker revealed that, over the years, these six men had endured just about everything a person can experience in life—losing jobs and raising children, starting businesses and finishing marathons. And now they were faced with one of the most difficult losses of all—one of their own. Jack would no longer be cracking corny jokes over pancakes in the corner booth at the diner. Praying for Jack's wife and adult children as he concluded, the speaker was overcome with emotion, and it was made all the more tender when the four other members of the group joined him at the podium and placed their hands on his shoulders.

At that moment, Ben could no longer hold back his own tears. How he longed for that kind of true friendship, that cord of connection with spiritual brothers who would encourage him and challenge him and hold him to the highest standard of Christ's example. But Ben had always been afraid to open up to friends— really open up—even when he had the opportunity. His wife was, of course, his best friend, but there were certain things that only another Christian brother could fully grasp.

Later, at the reception after the service, Ben introduced himself to the man who had spoken on behalf of the Super Six. Ben told him how lucky he was to be part of such a group. The man looked him in the eye, smiled, and said, "Well, we didn't just luck into being part of this group. We made a commitment to one another, one that God has blessed and used in our lives. He'll do the same for you if you'll let him."

The words haunted Ben for the rest of the week. He couldn't shake the feeling that God wanted him to do something. Finally, that weekend, he called two guys he knew from church, Kurt and Ron, and asked if they'd like to have breakfast the next Thursday. Both said yes.

6.1 Mother Knows Best

My mom used to share with me tons of her motherly wisdom, usually at what I considered to be the worst possible times. When our team lost a ballgame and I was feeling disappointed, she might say, "It doesn't matter if you win or lose; it's how you play the game." (Obviously, Mom had never watched her center fielder bobble a pop fly that cost her team the game.) Or if I got frustrated because I couldn't follow the directions for assembling a model plane: "You can do anything you set your mind to."

But the clincher, the one she told me most often, dealt with my friends: "You are who you run with." Sometimes I wasn't sure whether she was approving of my buddies or encouraging me to find better replacements. She probably wasn't sure either. What became clear, though, was the truth of her sayings. Whether you're a kid, a tween, a teenager, a young adult, or middle-aged, you *will* become like your closest friends. Count on it.

When we connect with another person, we become a conduit for their values, beliefs, and decisions. I'm not basing this just on my mom's apple-pie advice or on some clever pop psychology. In the Bible, Solomon wrote, "Walk with the wise and become wise, for a companion of fools suffers harm" (Prov. 13:20). If you stick close to people who are wise, you'll become wiser. If you hang out with people who are godly, you're likely going to grow closer to God. If you become close friends with people who make good decisions, chances are you'll make good decisions too.

But the opposite is dangerously true as well. If you hang out with the wrong crowd, you'll likely end up doing stupid and dangerous things along with them. If the people you surround yourself with are passive, unmotivated people, you'll likely do less, not more. If your best friends constantly ignore God, chances are you're going to drift from him as well.

When I reflect on my life, I realize I rarely got into trouble by myself. Almost every time I did something stupid or unwise, I was running around with people who were equally foolish. On the flip side of that coin, I rarely succeeded at anything on my own. If I did well in sports, I had a good coach helping me or teammates challenging me and cheering me on. When I grew as a leader, it was never in a vacuum. I was always blessed to have others speaking life into me and offering me valuable feedback. The same is true spiritually. Whenever I'm closest to God, I'm always simultaneously close to godly people as well.

Show me your friends, and I'll show you your future.

Any success I have in life is the direct result of a decision that changed the story I get to tell today. With God's help, I connected with the best, God-loving, wise people I could find. And once I started look- ing, God continued to bring them across my path. Anything good that I've done or am doing comes from

> Show me your friends, and I'll show you your future. The people you're hanging out with today are shaping the person you will become tomorrow.

God's using the right people to influence me and make me better. I am who I am today because of the friends I chose in the past.

You are too. The people you know determine the story you tell.

And the people you're hanging out with today are shaping the person you will become tomorrow.

6.2 BFF IRL

It's midnight, and you get that phone call every parent dreads, telling you your teenager has been involved in a collision and is being rushed to the ER. Or maybe it's that unexpected conver- sation with your boss when he informs you your position has been eliminated and you have until five o'clock to pack your desk and leave the building. It could be when your spouse tells you he's been having an affair, or when your test results come back positive for a disease you thought only other people got. Who do you call in those moments? Who do you want to confide in as you enter the valley of the shadow of life's most heartwrenching events?

Other than family members, most people either call a close friend or wish they had someone they could call. In those moments, we desperately need each other. We need someone who cares to be present with us, someone to listen to us vent or hold us while we cry. We need trusted friends to love us and remind us of God's peace and presence in the middle of life's unexpected storms. And not only do we need this type of friend, we need to be this type of friend to others, the kind other people trust and respect, confide in and love to be around.

But I fear such connections are becoming rare.

As a pastor, I often hear the secrets that people are afraid to tell anyone else. They tell me because they trust me, or because they decide it's safe because I'm a pastor. People often bare their hearts to me because they just can't keep it inside any longer, and they have no one else in their lives they trust enough to keep their secrets and to help them overcome whatever they may be facing. And that's a tragedy.

A number of years ago, I preached about secrecy and confession, and our church set up a temporary companion website. On this website, people could post their most carefully guarded secrets—anonymously. In the first two months alone, more than three hundred thousand people visited the site. Tens of thousands revealed the terrible burdens that were weighing them down, including sexual abuse, physical and domestic abuse, affairs, violence, and just about every addiction you can name.

While I was grateful that so many people had that opportunity to unload their heavy hearts, I was equally saddened that they felt they had no one with whom they could share those burdens.

I get it; there's no risk when you share something anonymously online. But any sense of relief you could get from something like that is temporary. People's lives are messy—mine, yours, everyone's—so if we're going to connect with others, we have to help each other clean up some of the messes. That's why it's absolutely essential to have real friends (and the right friends) in your life before your life derails in some way. Real friendships, though, take time, which is part of what makes it so difficult for us to connect.

Today it almost seems old-fashioned to hope for the kind of friendship that endures, the kind that sustains you through all the highs and lows of life. In our fast-paced, mobile culture, we've become suburban nomads. It's just not reasonable to expect relationships to last for years and years. Plus, we now have all kinds of great ways we can stay in touch: texts, emails, Instagram, Facebook, Twitter, and other social media. You can always skype or facetime with those long-distance friends, right?

But few do, and the connection is not the same.

The relational impact of social media and technology has redefined the word *friend*. Once upon a time, even just a decade ago, when someone said they were your friend, you both understood what that meant: you shared interests, understood each other's goals, and enjoyed doing life together. Things are no longer that simple. You can have dozens—even hundreds—of friends that you've never met IRL (in real life). They may follow you on social media, or vice versa, without really knowing who you are or what makes you tick.

As I'm writing this, the average American has more than

three hundred Facebook friends, but only two people that they consider close friends.[1] And this is one-third fewer friends than the average person had just twenty-five years ago.[2]

Also, according to the *American Sociological Review*, a quarter of Americans (that's about eighty million people) say they have zero—nada, goose egg, none at all—close friends.

Why the decline? I wanted to know, so I did some research online to find out. While there are all sorts of theories, I can summarize them with four main reasons that people have fewer friends now:

1. *People are working more.* The more hours people work, the fewer hours they relate socially. More and more people say their closest friends are those they work with because they're less able to develop or maintain friendships outside of work.[3]

2. *People are moving more frequently.* In our mobile economy, people don't stay in one place as long as they used to, so they aren't becoming as close as they once did.

3. *People are getting divorced more often.* One spouse gets the couch, the table, and the television, while the other gets the recliner, the refrigerator, the bed. Just as they divvy up possessions, couples often divide their friends, who tend to side with one over the other.

4. *People are talking more online and less in person.* While we know the benefits of social media, communicating online has many downsides as well (which I covered in my previous book, *#Struggles*). Many people carefully

filter what they share with others so they can present only their best selves, making it much more difficult to be authentic in their real-world relationships.

Even as most of us are engaged in far more online activity now, many of us are experiencing less personal intimacy. For example, many people, when their phone rings, don't answer, letting it go to voicemail instead. If the caller leaves a message, we may listen to it later, at our convenience, then reply with a text if we feel like it. That lets us stay in control of the "conversation."

> We're connected, yet we feel lonelier than ever.

And this is hitting us in too many ways to count. I know people who check their Facebook page in the middle of the night because they feel alone. They may have seven hundred Facebook friends, but not one close friend in normal life.

We're connected, yet we feel lonelier than ever.

Poverty used to mean only one thing. Now sociologists are acknowledging at least three types of poverty (and some list even more). The three divisions of poverty that I see mentioned most often are:

1. Material poverty: the lack of basic needs.
2. Spiritual poverty: the lack of eternal meaning.
3. Relational poverty: the lack of intimate friendships.

This third one seems to have taken many people by surprise. But if you think about it, you may realize that it's true of you as well. Something is wrong. Something is missing. You might even acknowledge that it isn't actually a something but a someone.

Based on where you are right now, the decision you most

need to make may be to connect. Because believe it or not, you could be one friend away from changing direction.

6.3 Magnificent Seven

The choice to connect with someone can produce benefits beyond our wildest dreams. For instance, for years I was blessed to have a unique friendship with an unusual guy, a man who changed my life and ministry forever. Lyle Schaller (who went to heaven just a couple of years ago) was around seventy-five years old when we met. Even then, he was a legendary church consultant, so far ahead of his time that many people thought he had a screw loose. Our church was less than two years old, and I was closing in on thirty the first time I got to have an in-depth mentoring conversation with Lyle.

At the time, our church was meeting in a small bike factory that we had converted into a makeshift church building. Because it was so small, we had to hold three services just to accommodate everyone who wanted to attend. (That's not saying it was a lot of people; that's saying it was a very small space.) When I spoke with Lyle, I was considering adding a fourth service, even though everyone around me said that was too many to even consider. And to be fair, in the mid-1990s, I didn't know a single Protestant church in America that had four weekend services, so this idea definitely seemed cutting edge.

But after I shared my vision for a fourth service with him, being as enthusiastic but mature as possible, my new older friend looked at me kind of sadly and said, "That's the problem with you young guys. You all think so small." Ouch. That was not what I expected to hear. I felt slightly offended, but certainly Lyle had my attention. He continued, "You shouldn't be thinking three or four services. You shouldn't be thinking four or five. You shouldn't even be thinking five or six. You should be thinking about doing *seven* services at your first location, and then seven at your second, third, fourth, and so on."

I didn't realize my mouth had been gaping open until I noticed that my tongue was completely dry. He made my head hurt. I was so confused, I'm not sure I could have even counted to seven. Was this old dude insane? *Seven?* Maybe people had been right about him. Maybe Lyle was crazy. Maybe he just didn't have his finger on the pulse of the church. Maybe I should politely thank him for his time and get up and make my escape.

But I couldn't leave. I was fascinated. I had to hear more. The more he talked, the more I realized that my new friend wasn't crazy. He could simply envision a future no one else could see. And he was right.

When I wrote these words, our church had 164 weekend services at twenty-five locations in seven states. By the time you read this, all three of those numbers likely will be higher. Many of our campuses offer eight weekend services in their particular buildings. A few have nine. That's a lot of people whom I'm privileged to serve. And we couldn't have done it without Lyle's foresight, vision, and encouragement.

One of my happiest memories of Lyle is of a phone conversation we had shortly before he passed away. I was thrilled to tell him we are doing eight services—not seven, as he had recommended. His end of the line was quiet. When he collected himself enough to speak again, I could hear the smile in his voice. "You know, honestly, I never would have thought eight was possible."

Through our laughter, I told him, "That's the problem with you old guys! You all think too small."

It took several years, even decades, before people saw the wisdom in Lyle Schaller's forward thinking. I miss him, but he left an enduring legacy. Without a doubt, churches around the world are better today because he invested in their pastors. Lives all over the world were eternally changed because of his influence. And for me, one conversation with one man changed my destiny and our ministry, while impacting tens of thousands of people.

Who's the Lyle Schaller in your life right now?

6.4 Put in a Good Word

When you decide to connect with people, you change the story you will tell one day. That's been true throughout history. Just consider the man who wrote more than one third of the New Testament, the apostle Paul.

Paul wasn't always a Christian. Before he was a follower of Jesus, he was Saul from a city called Tarsus, an angry guy who persecuted and killed Christians. If you don't like Jesus groupies, you would have loved Saul. But after taking the lives of those who believed that Jesus was raised from the dead, Paul became one of them himself.

His transformation was so big, so radical, so life-changing that Saul-turned-Paul immediately wanted to tell others about Jesus. The problem was that no Christians trusted him, for obvious reasons.

The gospel of Luke puts it simply: "When [Saul] came to Jerusalem, he tried to join the disciples, but they were all afraid of him, not believing that he really was a disciple" (Acts 9:26). You can't blame the disciples for their skepticism. I wouldn't want the guy who killed Christians last month leading my small group Bible study! Would you?

So Paul had a problem. He'd been transformed by the love and grace of Christ. Because of Jesus, Paul wanted to preach. He knew he was called by God to do so, but he didn't have an ounce of credibility with the people who had been following Jesus for a long time. So Paul reached out to anyone who would give him a chance to share his newfound passion and love for Jesus. Little did Paul know that his decision to connect wouldn't just change his story; it would add to God's Word and change history. You see, Paul was one friend away from altering the course of his destiny. And that friend was a guy named Barnabas.

Luke shows clearly how Barnabas lent Paul his credibility and put in a good word for him: "But Barnabas took him and brought him to the apostles. He told them how Saul on his journey had seen the Lord and that the Lord had spoken to him, and how in Damascus he had preached fearlessly in the name of Jesus. So Saul stayed with them and moved about freely in Jerusalem, speaking boldly in the name of the Lord" (Acts 9:27–28).

What happened? Barnabas staked his reputation on Paul's

conversion being real, not just some Trojan horse ploy to infil-
trate Jesus' disciples. Barnabas vouched for his new friend's faith
in Christ, telling the other disciples about the passion Paul had
when he preached about Jesus, something that's hard to fake.
Because of Barnabas, the other disciples gave Paul a chance.

One friendship.

One massive difference in Paul's life.

An even bigger difference in the world.

> **You may be one friendship away from changing your destiny. You may be one connection away from changing the world.**

You may be one friendship away
from changing your destiny if you'll just
decide to reach out and connect with the
right people.

You may be one connection away from changing the world.

6.5 You're the One

As you consider what it might mean to risk connecting with people,
to reveal your heart, your real struggles, and your crazy dreams,
consider the three types of friends everyone needs to reach their
God-given potential: (1) a friend to challenge you and bring out
your best, (2) a friend to help you find strength in God and to grow
in your faith, and (3) a friend to tell you the truth, especially when
you don't want to hear it. To illustrate these three types, let's look
at the life of David in the Old Testament to see the people that God
used to make him the man God wanted him to be.

First, everyone needs a friend who makes them better, and
makes them want to be better. You don't have to know much

about David's life to know he was far from perfect. But even with all his mistakes, sins, and shortcomings, David was still described as "a man after God's own heart." (See Acts 13:22.) If you study David's life, it becomes clear that the right people at the right time helped him become the right man.

Although David had many people who made him better, I'd like to start with Samuel. During the time when God rejected Saul as the king (and this is a different Saul than the one we talked about earlier—what is it about that name?), God chose Samuel the prophet to identify and anoint the next king of Israel. When Samuel visited the house of Ben Jesse (David's dad), he saw an obvious candidate. The oldest son was strong, handsome, and qualified. Samuel thought that surely this man was God's chosen king. But God told him not to consider his stature, because God doesn't look at the same things people look at. Most people judge others by their appearance, but God looks past their appearance and into their heart (1 Sam. 16:7).

> Everyone needs a friend who makes them better.

When all the obvious sons turned out not to be God's chosen one, they finally called in the least likely one, the youngest, who was out tending sheep. And God spoke to Samuel and said, "Rise and anoint him; this is the one" (1 Sam. 16:12). Everyone would have been shocked by this announcement. David was just a kid, and a little rough around the edges, camping next to his family's flock of sheep. There wasn't a single person in David's family who would have picked him as the next king. But God used one man, Samuel, to help David see that God's will for his life was more significant than anyone could have imagined.

Samuel made David better—much better. The prophet helped David see himself the way God saw him—as a leader, warrior, poet, and king. He wasn't just some kid, cut out for nothing more than wrangling sheep his whole life. Samuel told David, "You're the one! God has chosen you!" God had a glorious plan, and Samuel helped David glimpse it.

Do you have a few friends who make you better, people who see your potential for royalty? Think about it. Do your buddies at the gym make you better? Or the ladies in your reading group help you grow? Do the people you work with make you sharper? Do the moms you run with make you stronger?

If not, connect with someone new, someone who makes you better.

Years ago I made friends with a guy at my gym named Bart, who has helped me change my body in more ways than I can count. I had worked out for most of my life, exercising faithfully for more than twenty years. But I also ate whatever I wanted. And by whatever I mean anything with sugar or salt (and especially sugar *and* salt): donuts, cinnamon rolls, cake, ice cream, candy bars, chips and salsa, chips and dip, chips and cheese, and chips and whatever was within reach that I could dip them in.

But I was one friend away from changing my physical future. I noticed that Bart didn't work out much harder than I did, but he looked very different than I did. He was ripped! I always attributed that to genetics, but Bart helped me see that diet is actually just as important as exercise. Little by little, he helped me make small changes. First I added protein. Then I cut carbs. Then I added vitamins. Then I cut down on desserts. And together we tweaked my workouts. Over time, I became stronger and leaner, and I felt better. But more important, I was healthy, probably healthier than I've ever been.

One friend.

Too many changes to count.

If you need to get closer to God, connect with the right person who can help. If you want a good marriage, there's nothing like befriending people who have strong marriages. If you want to grow in your parenting skills, you might find someone wise and do life with them. Walk with the wise and grow wise. If you hope to start a business, then gleaning from someone who started a successful business is a great place to start. If you need to learn to handle your finances better, I know that if you pray for the right influence, God will answer that prayer.

David's son Solomon, the wisest man who ever lived, said, "As iron sharpens iron, so a friend sharpens a friend" (Prov. 27:17 NLT). Instead of hanging out with people who dull your skills or put down your dreams, it's time you start finding friends who make you sharper. If you connect with someone who makes you better today, the stories you tell tomorrow will become even more meaningful to you and others.

Who sees you, the real person inside you, the way God sees you?

6.6 Safe Places

The second type of friend can help you find strength beyond yourself in the midst of temptation and weakness. Just as Samuel helped David see that God wanted to do more in his life than he ever imagined, a guy named Jonathan helped David find strength in God when he needed it most. David was chosen to be the next king, but God didn't promote him to the throne immediately. God still had a lot to do before he replaced Saul with David. First, David became a war hero, winning the hearts of thousands. David was so effective on the battlefield that women danced in the streets singing, "Saul has slain his thousands, and David his tens of thousands" (1 Sam. 18:7). You can just imagine how jealous that made an already insecure king. Feeling threatened by David's rising popularity, King Saul plotted to take his life. David was forced to flee to the mountains to hide from the raging monarch's posse.

There, in David's darkest moments, God sent him an unlikely friend to help him find spiritual strength. King Saul's own son Jonathan recognized the error in his father's ways and stood faithfully by his friend David. Here's how Samuel describes the courageous show of support: "While David was at Horesh in the Desert of Ziph, he learned that Saul had come out to take his life. And Saul's son Jonathan went to David at Horesh and helped him find strength in God" (1 Sam. 23:15–16).

I love that simple phrase, which describes so clearly one of the key ways Jonathan served David: he "helped him find strength in God." There may not be a more valuable gesture one friend can make to another than pointing them toward God, encouraging them to seek his power, loving them toward God's unending strength.

I learned this truth years ago when I was young in ministry.

By the power of his grace, God helped me make a connection that changed my life. As a twentysomething pastor, I was so young and insecure that I always felt unqualified to fulfill my calling. It felt like I spent half my time trying to reassure myself that I could actually be a real pastor.

One day a guy from church invited me to lunch. I didn't know John well, but I'd already heard a lot of good things about him from other people. Of course, I had no way of knowing that one day fifteen years later I'd push him down in a back yard to get away from a psycho killer dog. (But that's a story you already know.) When I accepted, I assumed that, like most other people who called me for lunch, John wanted to talk about some problem or spiritual issue in his life.

When we sat down across from one another, we started in with the polite small talk two guys do when they don't know each other well. But as soon as the waiter walked away after bringing us our food, John's tone changed, hinting at the real reason he had asked me to lunch.

John said thoughtfully, "Do you mind if I ask you a question?"

Here it comes, I thought, imagining the possibilities. *What do I do if I'm doubting God? How do I know if I'm really saved? I'm trying to make a big decision, but I'm wondering, how do I know what God's will is for my life?*

But John didn't ask anything for himself. He asked me, "Who are you able to open up to? I know people come to you with problems all the time, but I was wondering, who do you have that you can go to for help?"

"Um . . . well . . . wow. I didn't expect that," was about all I managed to get out. My mind raced for an answer, any answer. *There's . . . well, let's see . . . I mean, I talk to Amy, of course. And then there's . . . hmmm.* When I couldn't come up with anyone, I tried to deflect his question with a poor stab at humor. "Well, I have a whole church full of people who are there if I need them," I said through a smile, unconvincingly.

What John said next was the start of a crucial twenty-five-year (and counting) friendship during which he has tirelessly helped me find strength in God. "Well," he said casually, sincerely, "if you ever need a safe person to talk to out of a whole church full of people, I hope you'll call me first."

And so I did.

It would be impossible to count the number of times over the years that John (who's the first to admit he's far from perfect) helped me find strength in God. What's interesting as I reflect on it now, though, is that I don't know that John has ever once given me direct advice. He simply listens to how I'm struggling, then asks me great questions. That's what he's always done. If I'm furious and want to call someone to give them a piece of my mind, he asks me what I think is the wisest thing to do. If I'm hurting, he asks me how I think Jesus might respond. If I have a big decision to make, John asks me what advice I'd give myself. If I'm discouraged and feel like giving up, he asks me if I really believe God is through with me. No matter what, John always covers my back in prayer, providing me with a safe place to recover, refocus, and regroup.

Time and time again, this one friend helps me find strength in God.

I talked to a guy just yesterday who is at the top of his game professionally. He's as successful as any guy could want to be in his career, but he told me he's failing in his personal life. I asked him, "Who do you have in your life that encourages you spiritually?" Holding back tears, he looked at me as though I had just asked him, "Who flies you to the moon on their own personal rocket ship?"

"I don't have any idea what that would look like," he said to me. He thought for a second, and I thought I saw a glimpse of hope in his eyes. "But if you know someone who could help me like that, I'd love to talk to him."

And that was that. I looked at this guy and told him that his story was about to change. I offered to be the first person to help. And then I made a phone call to a buddy who has a heart to help successful men who are struggling. And these two guys will be meeting later this week. It's too early to tell, but I've seen it hundreds of times before. This could be a friendship that changes this guy's destiny.

Who helps you find strength in God? If you don't have anyone, it's time for you to connect with someone who can help. God already has that person ready for you. It's not a sign of weakness to ask for help. It's a sign of wisdom.

> It's not a sign of weakness to ask for help. It's a sign of wisdom.

6.7 Let Me Put It This Way

Everyone needs a friend who helps them get better. And we all need someone to help us find strength in God. The third type of friend that we must have is one who will tell us the truth—the whole truth, God's truth, the truth that brings a reality check. And the more successful you become, the more you need this person in your life and, oddly, the harder they are to find.

King David discovered this the hard way. During the season when kings were supposed to be at war, David decided to stay home rather than go to battle. One night he was out on his rooftop when he saw his neighbor's wife, Bathsheba, bathing outside her house. His selfish lusts spoke louder than his wisdom, so the king sent someone to bring the woman to him. What's interesting is that whomever King David sent to get Bathsheba had to know that she was married to Uriah, one of David's closest friends and one of Israel's greatest war heroes. But since the messenger was on the king's payroll (and he might have been afraid of losing more than just his job), the guy did exactly as he was told. He summoned the woman to the king's palace. And if you don't know the story, well, one thing led to another, and Bathsheba ended up pregnant.

Recognizing that this could become a scandal, David tried to get control of the situation. He called her husband home, figuring Uriah would sleep with his wife and then assume the baby was his. But when Uriah refused to enjoy intimacy with his wife while his men were still on the battlefield, David changed his tactics. He issued the order to move his friend to the front line where he was sure to be killed. And he was.

Unfortunately, everyone in the king's court was too afraid to tell David the truth. So God sent a man who cared enough to help David see the way back to the right path. The prophet Nathan met with David and told him a story that went something like this: "Once upon a time there were two men. One was very rich and the other very poor. The rich guy had an unlimited number of sheep and wealth. The poor guy had almost nothing and only one lamb, who was almost like a pet to him and his family. When the rich man had a guest come to town, he took the poor man's lamb and had it butchered for their meal."

When David heard this story, he was beside himself with anger. David ranted, "As surely as the LORD lives, the man who did this must die! He must pay for that lamb four times over, because he did such a thing and had no pity" (2 Sam. 12:5–6). Fortunately, Nathan loved David enough to tell him the truth. "Then Nathan said to David, 'You are the man!'" (2 Sam. 12:7). That was enough to jolt King David out of his denial and bring him to his knees in repentance before God.

Many people around us tell us the things we want to hear, rather than helping us to see the truth. And the more successful we become, the more difficult it is to find people who have our best interests at heart. That's one reason we must connect with people who love us enough to be blatantly honest.

Amy and I have been blessed with a small group of friends that we've met with for more than twelve years. Even though they love us as their pastors, they also love us enough to shoot straight with us. This small group of people helped me in a big way many years ago. At the end of a Bible study, one of the guys joked about how I wasn't great at talking to people one on one. Everyone laughed, including me, but his tone had a serious edge. One of the ladies agreed that I came across as warm, fun, and likable when preaching, but that in person I seemed more distant and often distracted, even preoccupied. Suddenly, it wasn't so funny anymore. Then she asked if they had permission to help me see how I might be coming across to others.

Because I love and trust all of these people, I said yes. And because I gave them that permission, they were able to help me understand how I looked when talking to others. They told me the truth, even though it was hard for me to hear. Evidently, in the lobby between church services, I wouldn't always make eye contact with people, my eyes scanning the crowd instead. When they brought it up, I knew they were right. I was always trying to assess how many people might need my attention during that break so I could budget my time before the next service started. What I had thought was wise was actually coming across as rude and disinterested.

And that was only the beginning. I learned a lot about my interpersonal weaknesses that evening, things I sincerely needed to hear. My type-A, get-it-done mindset often left people feeling less than valued. In my heart, I knew that I cared about people, but my body language was saying otherwise. What's strange is that I had no idea this was happening. I thought I was great with people. Little did I know that many people were tolerating my shortcomings and not really enjoying my company.

To this day, I am overwhelmed with gratitude for my friends' honesty. I have worked hard to overcome my selfish tendencies and to consistently demonstrate value and care for whatever people I happen to be with. I try to be all there with them, fully present in the moment. Although I still need to improve, I'm now able to let go of distractions and engage with someone when we talk. I value and respect people, and I hope that they can feel it. None of these changes would have been possible without trusted friends loving me enough to do the hard thing and tell me the truth.

David's son Solomon wisely said, "An open rebuke is better than hidden love. Wounds from a sincere friend are better than many kisses from an enemy" (Prov. 27:5–6 NLT). When was the last time a friend loved you enough to give you an open rebuke? Has someone loved you enough to offer helpful correction? If not, you might be missing one or two very important relationships that could help you grow, thrive, and succeed. Everyone needs people in their lives who will candidly tell them the truth. Maybe you need to connect with someone who's willing to show you what you need to see so you can become the person you're supposed to be.

Which kind of friend do you need most in your life right now? Someone who helps you be better? Someone who helps you draw closer to God? Or someone who tells you the truth about yourself? Write your answer in a notebook or on a sheet of paper.

Is one person's name popping into your head right now? Someone you could consider getting to know better and sharing your need for this kind of connection? If not, ask God to provide the right person at the right time, that friend who can help you grow closer to him and to make decisions leading you in a divine direction.

> Everyone needs people in their lives who will candidly tell them the truth.

6.8 One Away

I'm guessing you would agree with my mom that you become like those you run with. Many sociologists say that you eventually become the average of your five closest friends. Your morals will be similar to your five closest buddies' morals. Your finances will look a lot like those of the people you spend the most time with. Your spiritual passion (or lack of it) will be similar to those who have the most influence on your life.

Keeping this in mind, ask yourself, "Who am I becoming?"

Be honest. Be Nathan for yourself. Is one or more of your closest friends battling with dangerous addictions? Are they struggling financially? Living risky lives? Making bad decisions? Are their relationships toxic? If so, you're either right there with them or on your way.

On the other hand, are you surrounded by people who know and love Christ deeply? Are they blessed and generous? Do they have positive, faith-filled perspectives on life and on the future? Are their relationships thriving? Are they using their influence to help make the world a better place? If so, praise God! You're likely seeing many of those same blessings in your life as well. You have so much to give to others who want to connect and discover all that God has in store for them.

Regardless of where you see yourself, I encourage you to take an inventory of your friendships. Which of your friends are close enough to you, intimate enough with you, that you would want them to speak at your funeral someday? Who would you want describing the special, close bond you shared and telling others about how you helped each other love and serve the Lord more completely?

You're one friend away from a better marriage.

You're one confession away from overcoming an addiction.

You're one conversation away from getting in better shape.

You're one introduction away from climbing out of the doldrums.

You're one mentor away from exercising your gifts and becoming a better leader.

It's not too late to connect with someone who will change your destiny. Your decision to connect will change the story you tell one day.

7 Trust

*When you can't see God's
hand, trust his heart.*

—EMILY FREEMAN

*E*mily couldn't believe what she had let Brad talk her into try-ing. Sure, they had been dating six months, but this next step required a level of trust that certainly would test their growing relationship. Did she love him? She wasn't sure. Yes? Maybe? She didn't want to run ahead of God and let her feelings dictate how she saw Brad. But clearly there was something special about him.

So as crazy as it felt, she had agreed to try something he loved passionately—rock climbing. It wasn't enough for him to risk life and limb by clambering up sheer stone walls; he wanted her to experience it with him. After much discussion, with lots of what *she knew were probably stupid questions, she surprised them both when she agreed.*

It wasn't that Emily didn't love adventure or taking risks. But she had always thought of herself as down to earth, not just figuratively but literally. Rock climbing was going to stretch her. Heights made her nervous, made her feel like she was losing control the higher she went. As a novice, she knew she was going to have to rely on Brad's expertise. He clearly knew what he was doing. Even better, he had proven to be a patient teacher when they came to the indoor climbing wall week after week to practice. But now she was trusting him with her safety, with her comfort level—with her life, for heaven's sake.

Before her first climb, they had shopped together for carabiners and snacks, and shoes for her, and she joked, "Wow. Rock climbing feels like such a major commitment!" She had regretted it instantly, not wanting Brad to feel that she was pressuring him about any kind of commitment. They had talked only vaguely about marriage, and really more around the idea of it. She felt they might be on the same page, but clearly he wasn't in any hurry.

"It is, Em," he had replied soberly. "Climbing requires a level of trust that's like getting married. You're sharing an experience with someone and relying on them completely—well, and God, of course." They had both felt awkward then, letting the moment pass, with Brad changing the topic to new Power Bar flavors.

But Emily hadn't been able to stop thinking about what he had said. What if rock climbing was about more than just rock climbing? What if it was about her future with Brad? She had a feeling God was about to take her higher off the ground than she had ever been.

She was going to have to trust him.

7.1 Stormy Weather

I live in Oklahoma, where the weather can change dramatically very quickly. One year in March, we had the most beautiful sunny spring day, with a high of 83 degrees. The very next day, it snowed three inches. And as dramatic as that change was, that's nothing compared with tornado season. You can enjoy a nice lunch picnic at the park, then a couple of hours later you're seeking shelter from a life-threatening twister. Storms seem to swirl up out of nowhere.

Just like they do in our lives.

My pastor used to always say, "You are either coming out of a difficult season in life, in the middle of a difficult season, or about to go into one." That may not be particularly encouraging, but I have to admit, it seems to be true. Life is difficult. Even when we're not in a rough season, it seems like there are often others close to us who are.

Even as I'm writing this, my family is facing some challenges. My mom's husband of the past fourteen years recently passed away. It was tough for all of us, but the hardest thing was seeing my mom grieve. She alternated between smiling and telling her favorite stories about Jack one moment, and then crying and wailing with grief the next, trying to accept that she'd never again wake up with him by her side. Then a close family member just called with bad news from the doctor. We're hoping that either God will heal him or the planned surgery will solve the issues he's battling. At the same time, one of my kids just went through a painful trial, and a precious gal in my office at church lost a baby during the first trimester of her pregnancy.

Life is tough.

If you (or someone you care about) isn't facing some real challenges right now, you should probably pause to enjoy it while you thank God. The truth is, in this sin-stained world, the painless times don't seem to last very long. When life gets tough, and we know it will, how we respond can either build our faith and draw us closer to Christ or weaken our intimacy with him as we slide in the wrong direction.

I talked to a lady at my son's soccer game yesterday who's been battling some health issues. She explained how she was close to God years ago and used to be very involved in our church. But when she started going through "the fire," she questioned why God would allow it. I could tell she was a little embarrassed to be talking to me about it, and she fought back tears as she said, "How can I worship a God I can't trust?"

Her question hits at the heart of one of life's biggest decisions. Will we trust that God is good even when life is not? Our response to pain and challenges determines so much about our future. If we decide to trust, we will grow in our faith, deepen in our intimacy with God, and be conformed to the image of Christ. But if we allow our hearts to drift, we'll wake up one day drowning in doubts, buried in burdens, and feeling far from the only one who can help us heal.

> Will we trust that God is good even when life is not? Our response to pain and challenges determines so much about our future.

The way we respond to challenges determines the stories we'll tell one day. Your decision to trust God in life's storms may be one of the best ongoing choices you ever make.

7.2 Does This Look Straight to You?

As a pastor, I'd argue that one of the most important challenges people face may also be one of the least talked about in churches today: doubt. Many sincere Christians battle spiritual doubts at one time or another, but few people feel comfortable talking about it with other believers. It's almost as if it's a sign of weakness, a lack of faith or commitment to Christ.

Some people say with confidence, "The Bible says it. I believe it. That settles it!" One guy I knew always used to say, "My faith is talking so loud right now I can't hear any doubt."

But that's not most people's experience.

And it's not mine.

For every person who has a genuine, rock-solid faith, I know ten more who are naturally skeptical. They are often thoughtful, intelligent, analytical people who *want* to trust God with everything in their lives. It's just that they need to settle a few issues before they can. Honest skepticism is not a bad thing.

Most of us begin this questioning process during childhood as we shift from believing everything our parents and teachers have told us to testing their wisdom with our experience. I remember sitting in church as a kid, bored as usual. That particular Sunday I had already drawn a Superman picture all over the offering envelope. We had just finished verse four of the last of the obligatory hymns. (We always sang verses one, two, and four. To this day I have no idea why we always skipped verse three.) And then our pastor, smiling and draped in a robe, stepped into a pulpit the size of a parade float and presented his sermon on that day's Scripture passage.

For whatever reason, something suddenly didn't seem right. I had walked into church that morning convinced that God was real. And then while I was listening to the sermon, questions flooded my mind: *What if all this God stuff isn't true? What if we're just imagining that there's a God? What if there is a God, but he's not the one we're worshiping in this church? What if everyone here just believes in God because that's what most Americans are conditioned to believe? I used to believe in Santa Claus, the Easter Bunny, and the Tooth Fairy, and look where that got me.*

Don't get me wrong. It wasn't like I was a Christian one moment, then an atheist the next. I still *wanted* to believe in God; it just got more difficult. The dam of my childhood acceptance gave way to my curiosity and cognitive development, which forced me to consider what was true for myself.

So I did what any eight- or nine-year-old would do. I tried making deals with God. Hey, I'd been paying attention to how things worked. From Sunday school, I knew Moses got a burning bush. David got some help with a lion and a bear and a really big guy named Goliath. And Shadrach, Meshach, and Abednego didn't burn in the fiery furnace. So I decided that God could give me a little something to help me believe.

It seemed only fair.

Since I wasn't one of the Bible heroes listed in Hebrews 11, it didn't seem right to ask for something massive. I didn't ask God to make the sun stand still or to send animals two by two into my bedroom to prove that he was real. No, I simply went to a picture on my wall and adjusted it from hanging straight to being slightly crooked. Don't ask me why that's the fleece I chose.

Then I had a quick conversation with the all-powerful God of the universe that went something like this: "God, I want to trust you, but I'm not sure whether you're real. So I just moved that picture on my wall so it's hanging crooked. Would you straighten it for me while I'm asleep? When I wake up and you've done that, I'll know you're real, and I'll serve you for my whole life." That seemed like a simple request, easy enough for the all-things-are-possible-with-God God.

The next day, the picture was still crooked.

To say that I was devastated would be an understatement. I was convinced that I had made a fair and pathetically easy-to-do request. I knew God doesn't sleep, but still, he could have done my request in his sleep, easy peasy. And yet the picture wasn't straight.

So I did what many people seem to do. I tried to bury my doubts.

The only problem was they didn't stay buried.

I wanted to trust God completely, but I couldn't.

Doubt—or the absence of trust—comes in all shapes and sizes. Some people might doubt God's very existence. Others believe he is likely real, but just not very involved in our everyday lives. Some might not trust his goodness, arguing that if God were truly good, then he wouldn't allow so much evil and suffering in the world. Some might not pray often or ever, doubting that their prayers make any difference at all.

Is God there?

Is he real?

Is he good?

Is he involved?

Does he even care?

Some people argue that if you have any type of doubt, then you don't have strong faith. I'd suggest looking at it from a different angle: you might not have strong faith unless you push through some honest doubts.

In order to decide to trust, you have to let yourself doubt.

7.3 Trusting Thomas

Many people struggle to trust God fully because they want a logical, rational approach to life. They're looking for something scientific, verifiable, and consistent that can support their faith. But by its very nature, faith requires trust in something—or in someone—that's not always predictable or understandable by human standards. Even if you're not wired this way, surely you can understand the desire to have irrefutable proof of God's benevolent presence in our lives.

Wanting proof is nothing new. Even if you don't know much about the Bible, chances are you've heard of Doubting Thomas. It's interesting to me that there are only twelve verses in Scripture that mention Thomas, and yet he's been labeled for centuries as one of the world's biggest doubters when, in reality, that was only a very small portion of his story.

The rest of Thomas's story gives us hardcore evidence that great doubters can become people of great faith. After Jesus died on the cross and rose from the dead, Thomas said he wouldn't believe it unless he saw proof. And instead of getting mad at him and casting him aside for his lack of faith, Jesus gave Thomas exactly what he needed to believe: "Put your finger here; see my hands. Reach out your hand and put it into my side. Stop doubting and believe" (John 20:27).

Perhaps in this season of your life you can relate to Thomas's longing for certainty. You don't understand everything about God. Some things in your life aren't adding up. You have questions. Lingering doubts. Some spiritual reservations.

You may even believe in God, but you just don't trust him completely.

You may even be committed to following Jesus, yet you still hold back some part of yourself, wondering whether God really has your best interests at heart.

Thomas learned the same answer you might experience. There is a difference between believing *in* and believing. Thomas believed *in* Jesus. But once he touched his Lord, once he had his questions answered, once the tension was resolved, Thomas no longer believed *in* Jesus. He believed him.

Consider the way Thomas's trust and faith in Jesus dramatically changed the story he would one day tell. If he continued to doubt, Thomas's story could have gone something like this:

It's true that I was one of the twelve that Jesus chose to follow him as his disciples. And I saw things that are still hard to believe. I saw Jesus open blind eyes, heal deaf ears, even raise the dead. But his miracles weren't even the best part. His love was indescribable. Jesus loved people everyone else hated. I mean, he really loved them. And his teaching was . . . it was like it came straight from heaven. So you can imagine how devastated I was when the Roman soldiers took him and beat him. Knowing he suffered as he did was too much to bear. But that isn't what killed me. When he died, all the hope I had died with him. Sure, the other guys claimed he rose from the dead, but I just didn't believe it. Peter still is preaching about it. James is actually running the church. John won't shut up about his love. But me, I just went back home. I wish I believed he was back, but I don't.

But this is not Thomas's story. The one-time doubter became one of the most faith-filled believers. Thomas was so convinced that Jesus had risen that he left his comfortable surroundings and traveled all the way to India to tell people about Jesus. He's known as the first evangelist to take the gospel to this part of the world and to share it boldly. And when opponents of Christ threatened his life if he didn't renounce his faith, Thomas stood firm. As a result, the Christ haters drove a spear through his body, turning him into a faithful martyr of the gospel.

Thomas trusted Jesus enough to die for him. Do you trust him enough to live for him?

Doubting Thomas became Trusting Thomas, and it changed the rest of his story. His life teaches us that doubt is not the end of real faith but often the beginning. Thomas trusted Jesus enough to die for him.

Do you trust him enough to live for him?

7.4 Life Preservers

I've been married for more than twenty-five years now, and thankfully, I've learned an important lesson about how to respond when Amy's upset. Most of the time when my wife tells me about her struggles, she doesn't want me to fix them; she just wants me to care about what she's experiencing. Once I realized she didn't want me to brainstorm solutions or tell her how to fix her problems, it took a lot of the pressure off. She just wanted me to listen with my heart and care that she was hurting.

And women aren't the only ones who want to be heard in the midst of life's struggles. We all do. When life seems to turn upside down, it's only human to want to be reassured that everything's going to be okay. We knew that intuitively when we were little kids, and even though as we got older we learned to hide it and to defend our hearts, we still want to feel like our pain matters to someone. And I'm convinced that we long to believe it matters to God.

There's certainly evidence for this in the way the disciples responded whenever troubles came their way. One time Jesus and his disciples boarded a small boat to cross the Sea of Galilee. This little body of water is about 680 feet below sea level, surrounded by hills, the perfect environment for a storm to blow in without warning. And that's exactly what happened on their short trip to the other side. Mark wrote, "A furious squall came up, and the waves broke over the boat, so that it was nearly swamped. Jesus was in the stern, sleeping on a cushion. The disciples woke him and said to him, 'Teacher, don't you care if we drown?'" (Mark 4:37–38).

Now, I've heard some people criticize the disciples for their worry over the storm. Not me. I totally understand where they're coming from. When I'm flying, I'm not a big fan of turbulence. I was on a flight recently that felt more like a thrill ride than a commercial flight. If Jesus had been sitting next to me on this plane, asleep the whole time, I can guarantee you I would have woken him up. "Did you not feel that? Aren't you going to do something?"

We can see their lack of trust in the question they asked: "Don't you care if we drown?" In other words, "I'm trying to trust you, but our lives are in danger, and you don't even seem to notice. Here I've devoted my entire life to following you around, trying to learn to do things your way, yet you don't seem to understand me at all."

Have you ever talked to God like that?

Lord, don't you care that I'm hurting? Don't you care that all my friends are getting married and I'm still all alone? Don't you care that my grandma has cancer? Don't you care that my spouse is cheating on me? Don't you care that I've prayed for years and asked you to do something and you don't even seem to notice?

After the disciples expressed their fear and their lack of trust, Jesus got up and did something he did often. He performed a miracle. He rebuked the wind and the waves. He told the raging storm to "be quiet and still." And everything was instantly calm again. Then Jesus turned his attention to his disciples and asked one of the most important questions he could ever ask.

"Why are you so afraid? Do you still have no faith?" (Mark 4:40).

It was almost like he was saying, "Really? Don't you know me by now? Do you really think I'd let anything happen to you out here?" I wonder how many times Jesus might want to ask us something similar. "Why are you so afraid? Why do you doubt my goodness? Why do you try to do everything yourself? Why don't you trust me?"

So many people think that if you're a Christian, you shouldn't have trouble. If you're following Jesus, you shouldn't experience trials, right? Actually, that's dead wrong. Jesus even promised the opposite: "In this world you will have trouble" (John 16:33). Thankfully, he didn't end his promise there, adding, "But take heart! I have overcome the world."

If it's true that God loves us so much, why would he ever allow things to become more difficult for us? I certainly can't completely answer that question, but I do know this: when things are good, people tend to forget about God. I hate to admit it, but that can be very true for me. When everyone's healthy, when there's money in the bank, when all my relationships are moving smoothly, it's easy for me to start doing life in my own strength, letting my awareness that I need him fade. We think, *Things are good. Why do I need God now?* But the moment life throws us a curveball, God's the first one we turn to for help.

I had a really funny conversation with a lady one time on a plane. It's rare for me to have a meaningful conversation with a stranger I meet on a short flight. Once they find out I'm a pastor, they usually don't want to talk anymore or they suddenly turn on their religious talk, saying things like, "Praise the Lord, brother. I'm thankful to be flying close to the heavens where we'll soar the sky on wings like eagles. Glory be to God!"

So when I sat next to a lady who was very nervous about flying, I tried my best to develop a rapport with her without giving away what I do for a living. Sure enough, the moment she learned I was a pastor, she blurted, "I don't believe in God, and I don't want you trying to convert me!" After I promised I wasn't going to try to ensnare her in some "in-air evangelistic meeting," we settled into a pleasant conversation. Until, that is, we flew through some massive turbulence.

When I fly, I can weather most turbulence without panicking. This was different. We hit such a fierce pocket that the captain didn't even attempt to comfort his terrified passengers. We plunged so violently that several overhead bins burst open from the jolt. Many people screamed. Especially my new very-afraid-to-fly atheist friend.

This turbulence was so bad that I started praying not for our safety but for the forgiveness of my sins—just in case we died. For the record, I actually believe that my past, present, and even future sins are covered by the blood of Jesus. But this turbulence was so bad, I wasn't willing to take any chances. That's how scary it was!

Since the lady next to me didn't have any reason not to swear, she unleashed a tirade so raw, so primal, so loud that everyone on the plane could hear her. She lifted profanity to unrivaled poetic heights, introducing words I didn't know existed. She relented only once, taking a break between her profanities just long enough to lean toward me and shout, "I still don't believe in God, but while you're praying, you might as well pray for me too!"

It's easy to ignore God when life is good, but he sure seems appealing in the middle of a storm.

Jonah knew a thing or two about that. He'd rebelled against what God had told him to do and made a run for it in the opposite direction. But through a series of unusual events, Jonah's actions caught up with him at sea. He was thrown overboard and swallowed by an enormous fish. Jonah himself described the life-altering incident this way: "In my distress I called to the LORD, and he answered me . . . When my life was ebbing away, I remembered you, LORD, and my prayer rose to you . . ." (Jonah 2:2, 7). Notice when Jonah remembered God: it was during his distress. I can't think of many people who remember God during their success, but I know plenty who do during their distress.

When you're drowning, you need a life preserver. When there's a storm, you need shelter. When you're hurting, you need a comforter.

God allows storms in our lives for a variety of reasons, and one of them is to draw us closer to him.

> **When you're drowning, you need a life preserver. When there's a storm, you need shelter. When you're hurting, you need a comforter.**

7.5 Cash and Carry

Like Jonah, I didn't decide to trust God during the smooth times of my life. I learned to trust him when a storm was raging. What I'm about to tell you might not seem like a big deal to some people, but about ten years ago, I decided to trust God with one of my greatest fears. And surrendering this fear to him helped change the story I was telling.

Throughout my life, I've had an overwhelming fear that my family wouldn't have enough money to meet life's needs. To many people, this is an irrational fear, but to me it was paralyzing, almost daily having a negative impact on my life. Every time a new book I was reading promised some pending economic collapse, I'd soak it up like a sponge. While rational people laughed at Y2K, I bought water, canned goods, silver coins, and a generator.

Once it became obvious to me that this foolish fear was having negative consequences for my family and for the church I was trying to lead, I finally agreed to go to counseling for help. My excellent counselor quickly helped me uncover the origin of this lifelong struggle.

When I was a young boy, my grandmother was one of my biggest heroes. She shaped my life in mostly positive ways during my formative years. Although she taught me enough valuable lessons to fill a library, the bad experiences she lived through during the Great Depression planted a seed of fear in my mind. I can recall every detail of sitting on Grandma's front porch with her as cars passed by on the street. I was six or seven years old when Grandma's stories painted a vivid portrait for me of her family's life during the Depression. They struggled daily for food. If there wasn't enough for everyone, her mother simply went without. Even sharing a home with another family, they sometimes went weeks without heat because they didn't have money to buy heating oil. My imagination made a movie in my head of businessmen jumping from skyscrapers because they'd lost everything.

It wasn't all bad. Grandma gave me practical advice that could help me avoid the storms she and so many others had to endure. I would need gold and silver because you can always use precious metals as money. Paper money would be worthless. And debt was worse than death. Never borrow money. And oh, yeah, don't trust banks. Just because they're open for business today doesn't mean your money will still be there tomorrow.

I remember deciding at that very early age that I'd never let my future family suffer. I'd be wise. Prepared. And ready for the inevitable economic collapse. I can remember as far back as age ten doing whatever kind of job I could get to earn money. I started a mowing business. I learned magic tricks and did shows for birthday parties. In high school, I started a tennis camp. I would do almost anything to make some cash. I wasn't materialistic. It wasn't because I was unsatisfied, always wanting more. I was simply terrified of not having enough.

It's embarrassing now to describe how deeply this sickness affected me. I loved cheeseburgers, but for years, I ordered only hamburgers because cheese cost a quarter extra, and what if I needed that someday to buy bread? When we went to a drive-in movie, I climbed into the trunk and sneaked in to save two dollars. And when I did get cash, you can be sure I never put it in a bank. No, I had to keep it where I knew it was safe: between my mattress and box springs.

Sick, huh?

Thankfully, with counseling—and a lot of prayer—I made some progress, little by little. And in 2006 I made a decision that stretched me to trust God in this most vulnerable area, a decision that has truly changed the story I can now tell.

But it was far from easy.

7.6 Give It Away

Our church had grown big enough that people outside our church started asking to purchase our weekend messages. Back then, most large churches regularly sold their messages on cassette tapes for a considerable profit. That extra money could go to the church or to the pastor who created the sermons. The demand for our teaching grew so large, we started talking seriously about starting a whole department just to oversee selling our materials.

And that's when one of my close friends, a staff member named Bobby Gruenewald, asked me a question that crashed head-on into my deepest fear and changed my story: "What if, instead of selling our materials, we just, you know, gave it all away, like, for free?"

Bobby's simple question inspired my faith, even as I felt fear crashing over me like a wave. The opposite sides of my heart pulled so hard away from each other, I thought my heart might tear right down the middle. I realized that what Bobby was suggesting was the right thing to do and could be a game changer for the church world. But it was still terrifying.

In the back of my mind I had always known that selling messages could one day be a source of personal income. That idea had always helped soothe my greatest fear. But losing that comfort wasn't the only reason for my hesitation. A bigger reason wasn't as selfish or personal but was very practical. At the time, our church had more debt than ever (and you already know how I feel about debt). We were so strapped that we often barely made payroll. I felt daily pressure to make ends meet in the church. And this burden was taking its toll. So if we started giving away our sermons and other materials, I knew that thousands (or even tens of thousands) of people would want them. And it wouldn't be free to us. We'd have to pay to build some system—staff, equipment, storage, development—to give them away, just as if we sold them. It sure looked like a lot of money going in the wrong direction.

Suddenly I was faced with an extraordinary opportunity to do something incredibly generous. Something right. Something godly. Or I could shrink back and do what everyone else expected, what everyone else was doing.

I won't overspiritualize this and tell you that I faithfully sought God in prayer. The truth is I just decided to do what was right and then trust God with the results. We'd give our messages away, free to anyone who wanted them.

Now, here's what's amazing: the moment we made that decision, it seemed like God blessed our church with financial provisions in a way he never had before. During our first ten years, we had existed hand to mouth. We never had extra money. Most weeks were so tight I had knots in my stomach. But when we decided to trust God, it was almost as if he decided he was going to trust us. A couple of years passed and my fears started to ease.

Then in 2008, the very thing I had dreaded since childhood actually happened. Many economists labeled this time the Global Financial Crisis, considered by most to be the worst of its kind since the Great Depression in the 1930s. My fear became real. And I was leading several hundred employees dependent on the generosity of church members, many of whom had just lost their jobs.

The storm blew in out of nowhere. Just weeks before, most market analysts were optimistic about the economy and the future. Suddenly the stock market plummeted, unemployment skyrocketed, thousands lost their homes, and millions saw their retirement savings cut in half.

That was when the oddest thing happened to me. In the middle of this storm, I experienced the presence of God like I rarely had before.

I wasn't afraid. Not at all. Not even a little bit.

When the rest of the world seemed to panic, I had a supernatural peace that I still may never fully understand.

My whole life, I had lived in fear. And now I was living in faith.

Just like the disciples had to learn to trust Jesus in the boat, I had grown to trust him even more deeply than I realized. It dawned on me: my faith was not in what was in the bank; it was in who was in the boat.

My trust was in Jesus.

I've learned that I experience Jesus better in the valleys than I do on the mountaintops. Sure, I appreciate him when things are good, but I *need* him when I'm low. David walked through the valley of the shadow of death and said, "I fear no evil because you

> I've learned that I experience Jesus better in the valleys than I do on the mountaintops.

are with me." In the same way, I decided to trust God as my provider when I had nothing else to trust but him.

Now I have a different story. We love to say as a church that "we will lead the way with irrational generosity because we truly believe it is more blessed to give than to receive." One decade ago, we had ten locations and twenty-six million dollars in debt. As of today, we have twenty-five locations, and we don't owe a penny to anyone. Even better, we have had the honor of blessing tens of thousands of pastors and millions of people with free resources designed to draw them closer to Christ. In the last year alone, more than 180,000 churches have used free resources that we made available. Tens of millions of people received free messages. And to date, our free YouVersion Bible App has been installed on more than 250 million devices.

Just like Thomas, I could have continued to doubt, but trust changed my story. Just imagine how choosing to trust could change yours.

Because the decisions you make today determine the story you'll tell tomorrow.

7.7 Present in the Purpose

To trust God regardless of your circumstances, remember two things when you're caught in a storm.

First, God's presence is with you, no matter how alone you may feel. He is always with you. Mark wrote in his gospel, "A furious squall came up, and the waves broke over the boat, so that it was nearly swamped" (Mark 4:37). Notice this wasn't just a spring shower; it was almost too much for the small boat and the frightened disciples to handle. But even though the circumstances seemed too much to bear, the disciples were not alone. Mark states, "Jesus was in the stern, sleeping on a cushion" (v. 38).

Again, so many people think that they wouldn't be going through their struggles if God were really with them. But that's simply not the case. Having Jesus in the stern beside you doesn't mean the storm won't rock your boat. It just means the storm won't sink you. Never forget: he's with you, both in a spring shower and in the worst tornado imaginable.

I've heard it said that the simple presence of anything living may help you to live a longer life. The presence of a spouse. Or of a child. A roommate. Even a dog, a bird, a rabbit, a hamster, a fish, a ferret, a fern, a hedgehog, and possibly certain kinds of cats. (Just kidding. We all know nothing good comes from cats.)

> Having Jesus in the stern beside you doesn't mean the storm won't rock your boat. It just means the storm won't sink you.

The good news is that you don't have to depend on a pet or a houseplant. You have the Prince of Peace, the Lord of Hosts, the Divine Counselor, who will never leave you and never forsake you. Just as Jesus was with the disciples in the boat, he is with you in the storm. And because he is always good, you can trust him.

When the storm hits and your faith remains strong, people will ask you all sorts of questions:

- "How are you holding up so well?"
- "Why are you not freaking out?"
- "How is it that your world is falling apart, but you're keeping it together?"
- "How do you have so much peace in the middle of all this chaos?"

And you can explain that you're not doing it by yourself. You have help that others might not see. An invisible power gives you strength when you feel weak. You have God's grace, God's power, God's comfort, and God's presence.

I love the comfort we find in so many of the psalms. "God is our refuge and strength, an ever-present help in trouble" (Ps. 46:1). He is ever present, always with us, faithful to help in time of trouble. I also love David's rich perspective in the classic twenty-third Psalm, where he wrote poetically, "Even though I walk through the darkest valley, I will fear no evil, *for you are with me*" (v. 4, my emphasis). The reason David had no fear is because he trusted the Good Shepherd. And just like David, I would rather walk through the valley of the shadow of death with Jesus than stroll on the mountaintops without him.

Second, not only is God with you in the storms, he will also use them for his purposes in your life. No matter how terrible it may seem in the moment, God always has a higher plan and a good purpose because he loves you more than you can imagine.

Think about the story we've been talking about. Who decided to take that boat ride? Did you even notice that detail? It was Jesus. After teaching, Jesus said, "Let's go to the other side." Why did he plan this short trip? Because he knew that on the east side of the lake there was a man in need. So he loaded up his buddies and started the journey to go help this suffering person. And since Jesus was God in the flesh, he knew the storm would come. Going into the storm was always part of his plan.

Don't miss this: The disciples didn't experience the storm because they were *out* of God's will. The disciples experienced the storm because they were *in* God's will. Their ordeal wasn't some accident, some freak event that took Jesus by surprise. He knew the storm was coming. And he knew it would serve a higher purpose in the lives of those he loved.

Now, you might be asking, "Did God *cause* the storm?" That's a great question, and a fair one. You might ask that about some area of your life or about someone you care about. Did God cause me to lose my job? Did God cause me to get depressed? Did God cause this bad thing to happen? We need to be honest and admit that brilliant and sincere Christians passionately debate this question. Does God cause everything to happen, or does God simply allow some things to happen?

Some say that God never causes anything bad to happen. Since God is a good God, they suggest that he causes only good things, and all bad things come from our evil opposition. Others argue that God is so big and sovereign that he rules the whole universe and causes everything that happens on earth and in heaven.

Honestly, I don't know. I'm not God. I can't tell you whether God causes storms or just allows them. But one thing you can count on is this: God always *uses* storms. When we love him and we're pursuing his purposes, he's always working things out for our good (Rom. 8:28).

When we recognize this truth, we can decide ahead of time that no matter what happens, no matter what life throws at us, we'll trust God.

If you know that God is always with you and that he uses everything for your good, why are you so afraid?

Trust him.

The more you get to know God, the more your faith will grow.

7.8 More Than You Can Handle

Maybe you've heard well-meaning people say, "God will never give you more than you can handle." While this sounds good and it might feel right, nowhere in the Bible does it ever actually say that. I'm almost certain most people are misquoting 1 Corinthians 10:13 when they say this. That verse reads, "And God is faithful; he will not let you be tempted beyond what you can bear." Clearly, we see that God won't let you be *tempted* beyond what you can handle. But Scripture never says that God won't give you more than you can handle.

I'd argue the opposite. God often allows you to experience more than you can handle to teach you to trust and depend on him.

The apostle Paul learned this valuable lesson and recorded his findings in 2 Corinthians. We're not sure exactly what his ailment was, but Paul had what he called a "thorn in the flesh." Scholars have theorized for centuries about the possibilities for his pain, but the best we can do is guess. What we know is that Paul pleaded faithfully with God multiple times to take it away, yet God never did.

If ever there was a person who was worthy of this type of miracle, it was certainly Paul. He suffered immensely for the gospel, way more than most of us could ever imagine or endure. He had boundless faith in God, and he prayed with all his heart. If God was going to answer anyone's prayer with a miracle, it seems like this one should be a top candidate. Yet God allowed Paul to continue living with that thorn, whatever it was, something that seemed like it was more than he could handle.

Paul, rather than allowing this challenge to turn him away from God, decided instead to trust God and let it draw him closer.

Is there something in your life that seems almost too much to bear? It might be some chronic pain. Or a sick child. Or constant financial battles. Relational challenges, a tough marriage, or a dead-end job. Or any number of other painful possibilities.

Your response today will determine to some degree your future.

In the middle of Paul's pain, God spoke to him and offered him this promise: "'My grace is sufficient for you, for my power is made perfect in weakness.' Therefore I will boast all the more gladly about my weaknesses, so that Christ's power may rest on me. That is why, for Christ's sake, I delight in weaknesses, in insults, in hardships, in persecutions, in difficulties. For when I am weak, then I am strong" (2 Cor. 12:9–10).

God promised that his grace was enough.

Paul didn't need God to remove his problem. God's presence was all Paul needed.

Don't believe the lie that God won't give you more than you can handle. If you decide to start something new, chances are it's going to be more than you can handle. When God prompts you to go start something new, he will provide you with enough grace to handle what you can't handle. When he leads you to stop something you've done for years, it likely will be more than you can do on your own. So just admit it and ask him to help you. And when you're weak, he will be strong.

When you know you need to stay and it would be easier to go, God will have to help you do what you can't do yourself. And when God tells you to go when you would rather stay, he'll give you the faith to take that first step. When God wants you to serve in ways that make you feel like you're in over your head, he'll empower you to do what needs doing. And when he guides you to connect with certain people in your life, you can be sure he's going to use that connection to bless you both.

But never be afraid to move forward through a challenge, trial, or storm because it feels like more than you can handle. Think about it. The first time you provide a foster home for a child, that's going to be more than you can handle. If you have teenagers, they likely will be more than you can deal with at times. When your bills keep piling up and you don't have enough money to pay them, you're going to need God's help. When you get a bad report from a doctor, you'll need God's strength and presence to sustain you.

You might be tempted to think, *I need to be strong*. But the truth is it's okay to be weak. In your weakness, his strength will be all you need.

Whenever you face a storm, a struggle, some unexpected trial, just remember God will occasionally allow you to have more than you can handle. He will use trials to change you into the image of his Son and teach you to trust him. He will transform these obstacles into vehicles for his blessings.

That's what God did for me. God transformed my fear into trust. The fear of not having enough became a faith to give, and then to give even more.

Instead of putting my hope in the boat, my soul hoped in the Lord.

So what are you so afraid of? Do you still have little faith? Trust God with whatever you've been holding back. Trust him with your future spouse. Trust him with your children. Trust him with your career. Trust him with your health. Trust him with your finances.

Trust him without reservation.

Period.

Big Impact

One of my privileges as a pastor is being with people at the end of their stories. Sometimes I'm there with their family as they pass on from this world. Other times I'm asked to lead the funeral or memorial service that honors a person's life. What I've discovered is that no matter how someone tries to tell their story, in the end, your life speaks for itself.

Some funerals are an honor for me to do, an absolute blast. When I ask the family to describe their loved one, sometimes they laugh as they recall story after story of how much joy their special person brought into all their lives. Other times they shed tears of sorrow because of how much they're already missing them. Of course everyone grieves the loss of a loved one, but there's still something special about getting to celebrate a life that was well lived.

But some funerals are really tough. I'll ask the family to tell me about the person who's gone, and the room fills with an awkward silence. Instead of getting to hear how he loved people unconditionally or how she was always there for anyone in need, the silence just hangs in the air as people struggle to think of something—anything—they can say.

Finally, someone will speak up and say something like, "Well, you know, Grandpa sure loved watching college football."

Everyone breathes a sigh of relief, agreeing that yes, he did obsess about those games. Or maybe one will say, "She really enjoyed reading murder mysteries," and several others nod in agreement.

There's nothing wrong with football or mystery novels, but is that how you want to be remembered?

More than what mourners have to say about their loved ones, it's often the things that are not said that really stick with me. There are always stories. But there aren't always stories families want to tell—you know, the good kind, where the deceased left a positive impact an acre wide and miles long, touching the lives of everyone they met.

I know it's hard to imagine, but one day people are going to talk about you. And what I've learned from all those funerals is this: at the end of your life, those who loved you most won't talk about many of the things that consume your thinking today. So many of the things we strive for, chase after, and emphasize in our culture never get mentioned in those settings. I've never been at a funeral where the family passed around their deceased loved one's resume, reminiscing about each of their accomplishments. I've never once seen family pass around bank statements or stock portfolios. And as much as our culture applauds sports, I've never seen trophies or medals displayed next to someone's casket.

It's not what they did that mattered but who they were.

Their motives, their attitudes, their feelings—the kind of person they were—these are the things for which they're remembered. Funny stories about how they always did certain things in their own special way. Memories of how they offered encouragement, support, friendship, compassion, and love to family, friends, coworkers, communities. Testimonies about how their strength, courage, stamina, and faith inspired everyone around them. These are what define a person's story in the end.

Stephen Covey, in his leadership classic *The Seven Habits of Highly Effective People*, asks readers to think through how they want to be remembered when they die. While it may sound creepy or morbid or depressing, it's actually a quite liberating and life-affirming exercise. When we think about the kind of person we want others to remember us for being, it's much easier to work backward from our deaths to make the choices now that can help us grow into that person. When we know our destination, it's much clearer when and where we should start, stop, stay, and go.

Ultimately, we know that our stories don't have to end when we leave this life. When we experience the grace of God through Christ, we can live forever serving and enjoying God in heaven. And while I don't know for sure, that's when I think the stories that our lives tell will be taken to a whole new level.

> When we know our destination, it's much clearer when and where we should start, stop, stay, and go.

Because our stories are not just *our* stories.

Our stories are part of an even bigger story.

Every life is connected to so many others.

My story is connected to your story. All of our lives intersect with countless other lives in ways that we don't recognize or can't even imagine. But God knows the big story, the grand design that he's been authoring since the beginning of time. He knows how all the chapters fit together, how each of our stories unite in an epic like no other.

Imagine a person in heaven explaining how your life impacted them. How your story changed their story. I've heard someone speculate that in heaven we'll have a huge banquet, a crazy-joyful dinner party unlike any other. During the meal, one after another, each person will share their story, and we'll finally get to see how they all fit together.

A decision in college to study instead of going to a party led to meeting the person who introduced someone to their spouse. Meeting their spouse led to the creation of the new lives of their children, the beginning of a new ministry, a church that blessed countless lives. Someone's refusal to cheat at work caused them to lose their job but ended up awakening their boss's conscience, which caused him to go to church, where he accepted Christ. One woman's commitment to stay in her marriage influenced one of her friends to forgive her own husband and to fight for their marriage. On and on, the stories flow together, like beautiful streams, creeks, and tributaries all merging into a magnificent, mighty river of God's redemption.

So how do you want your part in that ultimate story to read? I know you don't want to live with regrets. None of us does. But most will. You may not like where your story is heading, but it isn't finished yet. It's not too late to change it. We've all made decisions we regret. We've all made mistakes and found ourselves wondering how we were going to keep going. But the good news—the essence of that ultimate epic I was just talking about—is new life. A fresh start. Rebirth. Resurrection. Grace.

God wants your story to be more than "happily ever after." He wants you to be fulfilled "eternally ever after." If you allow him, your story will become written in a language more meaningful, with themes more beautiful, than you could ever imagine.

Which reminds me of an extended conversation I recently had with Chris and Cindy Beall. Chris joined the staff of our church about fifteen years ago as a worship pastor. Tragically, six weeks into his new role at our church, we discovered that he had been having multiple affairs. You can imagine how devastated we all were—especially Cindy, who, like us, had no idea.

I never will forget the conversation I had with Chris at our church after he got caught in the web of his deception. With as much love as I could show, I explained to Chris the decision he made in the next few minutes could impact his future in more ways than any of us could ever know. At that moment, he stood facing two paths going in opposite directions. He could continue to lie and deceive, cover his tracks, telling half-truths and hoping for the best. Or he could come clean. He could open up, confess all of his sins, cry out for help, and with the grace of God rebuild his life, his marriage, and his ministry.

The choice was his.

The right choice was the more difficult one. Way more difficult. But as Jesus followers, we know it's best to choose hard over easy when hard is right.

Chris took a deep breath and started talking. He told me about more things he did wrong than I could have dreamed up on my own. He talked. And talked. And talked some more. Once he finished vomiting years of addictions, lies, and deceptions, he stopped and simply said something like, "That's it. That's my story. And I hate every part of it."

At that moment, I realized I was staring into the eyes of a man who'd just been fully truthful for the first time in who knows how long. As his pastor, I had the divine opportunity to offer hope: "And at this moment your story is starting to change. What once was will now be no more. God can give you a new story." I explained to Chris that I'd come across a Hebrew word, *shuwb*, that's often translated as "restore" but also means "to turn back," "to return," or "to make better than new." We asked God to make that a word for their marriage. Not only would their story be healed, but it would become better than they could even dream.

We prayed together and the journey began. After months of counseling and deep and personal pastoral care, Chris and Cindy slowly rebuilt their marriage. Eventually, because they allowed God to bring about restoration, we allowed Chris to rejoin our staff in a more entry-level role. As he continued to prove himself, we slowly promoted him. Over the years, Chris worked his way up to leading our largest church campus, and now he oversees several other campus pastors.

Just recently, Pastor Chris preached to our whole church and told his entire unedited story. I don't think there was a dry eye in the whole church as Chris explained the depths of his sin and the glory of his wife's forgiveness and God's grace. Then he closed out the message talking about *shuwb*, the Hebrew word we'd prayed about years ago. Chris gave God the glory that his story that was once full of darkness was now full of light and life. By the grace of God and his family's courageous decision, God gave them a story that was better than new.

What the enemy had meant for evil, God used for good.

And the same can be true for you. When you stand at the fork in the road, have the faith and courage to choose the hard path over the easy one when the hard one is right.

The choice is yours.

The time is now.

To step into your divine direction.

Acknowledgments

I'd like to express my deepest gratitude to all my friends who contributed to this book.

Dudley Delffs: You are an editing ninja. And you are a great friend.

David Morris, Tom Dean, John Raymond, Brian Phipps, and the whole team at Zondervan: Thank you for your commitment to meet the needs of people with content that honors Christ.

Tom Winters: Thank you for being in my corner. You're a great agent and friend.

Brannon Golden: My life is better because of your family. Thank you for helping to make my books what they could never be without you.

Jennifer McCarty and Adrianne Manning: You are both the best. The way you serve daily honors Jesus and blesses my family.

Amy Groeschel: I thank God every day he directed you into my life. You are my best friend forever.

Notes

1. Jeanna Bryner, "You Gotta Have Friends? Most People Have Just Two Real Pals," NBC News, November 4, 2011, http://www.nbcnews.com/health/health-news/you-gotta-have-friends-most-have-just-2-true-pals-f1C6436540.

2. Janet Kornblum, "Study: 25% of Americans Have No One to Confide In," *USA Today*, June 22, 2006, http://usatoday30.usatoday.com/news/nation/2006-06-22-friendship_x.htm.

3. Dean Schabner, "Americans Work More Than Anyone," ABC News, May 1, 2016, http://abcnews.go.com/US/story?id=93364&page=1.

Christian Atheist

Believing in God but Living As If He Doesn't Exist

Craig Groeschel

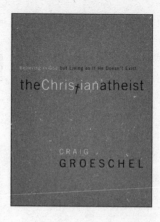

"The more I looked, the more I found Christian Atheists everywhere." Former self-proclaimed Christian Atheist Craig Groeschel knows his subject and his audience all too well. After several years of successful ministry, he had to make a painful self-admission: although he believed in God, he was leading his church as if God didn't exist.

To thousands of Christians and non-Christians across every town in the United States, the journey leading up to Groeschel's admission and the journey that follows from his family and his upbringing, to the lackluster and even diametrically opposed expressions of faith he encountered will look and sound like the story of their own lives.

Now the founding and senior pastor of the multicampus, pacesetting Life.Church, Groeschel's personal walk toward an authentic God-honoring life is more relevant than ever.

Christians and Christian Atheists everywhere will be nodding their heads as they are challenged to take their own honest assessment and ask the question, Am I putting my whole faith in God but still living as if everything were up to me?

Groeschel's frank and raw conversation about our Christian Atheist tendencies and habits is a convicting and life-changing read. This book is a classic in the making.

Available in stores and online!

ZONDERVAN®
.com

#Struggles

Following Jesus in a Selfie-Centered World

Craig Groeschel

The average person spends 7.4 hours a day staring at screens.

And that's just the beginning...

We all love the benefits of technology and social media, but even with the incredible upsides, many of us suspect there are unintended negative consequences of using them.

In this timely and life-changing book, Craig Groeschel, bestselling author and pastor of Life.Church, shows all whose digital dependency is becoming unmanageable how to regain control over their lives. He walks you through the biblical values that are essential for a life of peace and true fulfillment but are now even more important in our maxed-out, social-status-seeking world.

Groeschel also taps into some of the most up-to-date studies confirming the effects of social media on our emotions and our friendships. And he offers real-life examples of how we've come to rely on social media, how it masks our real struggles, and how we can reclaim a Christ-centered life.

Refresh and rediscover your understanding of the qualities that life with Christ brings: contentment, intimacy, authenticity, compassion, and rest. Ultimately, you will find *#Struggles* to be just the guide to bring a balance of spiritual depth and rich human engagement back to your everyday life.

Available in stores and online!

When a leader gets better, an organization gets better.

On the *Craig Groeschel Leadership Podcast*, Craig tackles some of the biggest issues facing today's leaders. Whether you're in charge or it's your first day on the job, you'll hear fresh ideas to guide how you lead at work, home, and beyond.

In each episode, you'll learn how to expand your capacity as a leader as Craig covers topics like:

- Leading up within an organization
- Sharpening your communication skills
- Institutionalizing urgency
- Creating a value-driven culture
- Effective time management
- And more!

Visit **www.life.church/leadershippodcast** to find your favorite way to watch or listen!

"Be yourself! People would rather follow a leader who is always real than one who is always right."—Craig Groeschel